P9-DDW-463

WOULD THE PILGRIMS STILL COME TO AMERICA TODAY?

The Deteriorating State of
Religious Liberty in America

NATE GRASZ

Foreword by
Lt. Col. Allen West

Endorsements

Religious liberty has never not been under assault, either by one creed seeking to exterminate all others, or by forces of secular absolutism, or in this age, by both. Every age needs new voices and new champions of the "first freedom," and Nate Grasz is one of those. In his eloquently and closely argued appeal for a renewal of commitment to religious liberty, Grasz lays down a marker for another generation of religious freedom defenders to follow.

~Hugh Hewitt, law professor, host of a nationally syndicated radio talk show

An eye-opening, at times shocking, look at how far we have strayed from the religious freedom that set America on the path to greatness. It is a blow to the Left's monopoly of politically-correct intimidation of Christians. A timely and timeless read.

~Nick Adams, Founder and Director of Foundation for Liberty and American Greatness (FLAG), media commentator, and best-selling author

Nate Grasz is an eloquent and fearless new voice from the millennial generation, summoning us back to the fundamental freedom of them all, religious liberty. If you believe as I do that America must remain a nation under God if she is to remain a nation at all, you must read this wakeup call for faithful patriots to act before it's too late.

~John Andrews, Founder of the Centennial Institute, former Colorado Senate President

The Pilgrims came to America to be free. They were determined to live in a place where their freedom of religion would not be at risk or be subject to the whims or preferences of government authorities. These admirable people have inspired generation after generation of those "yearning to breathe free." But now, as Nate Grasz eloquently points out, the government is constantly hectoring Americans to surrender their religious liberty rights. This book is a call to action by an outstanding young author who writes knowledgeably and with passion about the country he loves and the religious freedom he cherishes.

~Bill Armstrong, President of Colorado Christian University, former U.S. Senator

About the Author

A rising voice in conservative politics from the millennial generation, author Nate Grasz is a principled conservative dedicated to enhancing awareness, understanding, and thought-provoking discussion of important issues.

Nate has worked on various political campaigns and spent a year working as a program and policy analyst for the Centennial Institute, a prominent public policy think-tank dedicated to fostering faith, family, and freedom, before moving on to become an associate producer for the nationally syndicated radio program, *The Hugh Hewitt Show.*

Born and raised in Omaha, Nebraska, Nate is graduating from Colorado Christian University in December 2015 with degrees in Political Science and Business Administration, and is engaged to be married to his fiancé, Brenna.

Acknowledgments

Many thanks are due to those who helped make this book a reality:

To John Andrews, whose mentorship and guidance both during and after my time at the Centennial Institute provided me with the connections, opportunities, and experiences that made this book possible. Simply put, this book, as well as many of the best experiences I have had, would not have come to be without John Andrews.

To the Centennial Institute, Jeannie Edwards, Keri Brehm, Antonette Smith, and Allie Mahon. Their support and help reviewing this book is greatly appreciated.

To the various, greatly impactful professors I had during my time at Colorado Christian University. CCU is a special university that challenged me to think critically and helped shape my worldview. You won't find a university more committed to standing for the truth and fostering excellence in their students than CCU.

Special thanks are in order for my family: to my parents, Steve and Verlyne, my siblings, Caylen, Jackson, and Aubrey, and my fiancé, Brenna. Their continued love, support, and encouragement saw me through the completion of this project, and their assistance in researching, editing, and reviewing helped make this book a finished product.

Lastly, to Allen West, who first gave me the inspiration and encouragement to write this book. Allen West is a great man and a great American. His devotion to public service and fighting for conservative causes is truly admirable, and America is a better place because of it.

To my parents,
Steve and Verlyne Grasz,
and my best friend, Brenna.

Contents

11

"The Pilgrims came to America not to accumulate riches but to worship God, and the greatest wealth they left unborn generations was their heroic example of sacrifice that their souls might be free."

~ Harry Moyle Tippett

FOREWORD

By Lt. Col. Allen West

I met Nate Grasz at a retreat sponsored by the Centennial Institute of Colorado Christian University back in September 2014. He is one heck of a fella — astute, articulate, highly intelligent, and a committed Christian conservative. Nate seeks to promote faith, family, freedom, and future for the next generation of patriotic young Americans. His goal is to bring awareness, understanding, and thought-provoking discussion to important issues for millennials.

Indeed, would the Pilgrims want to come to America today? Or would they see it as the England they sought to flee because of religious persecution by the State? It is a very pointed question that, if you honestly assess, the answer is certain — they would not set sail for Plymouth Rock in these current United States of America.

And therefore, how long will it be before we forget the real story and lesson behind Thanksgiving? People seeking religious freedom from persecution — funny thing; where would we go today to find safe harbor to worship? Remember the first amendment says, "Freedom of religion and the free exercise thereof." I am thankful for the landing at Plymouth Rock, the desire of the Pilgrims to establish a sanctuary for religious freedom—and for our Founding Fathers who codified it.

But as Nate brings out — "when did atheism and religious intolerance become the official position of the United States?"

I do find it rather confusing that people claim offense by something they state does not exist.

Thanks, Pilgrims, for giving us Thanksgiving Day and our religious freedom.

Allen West is the President and CEO of the National Center for Policy Analysis, a Fox News contributor, Senior Fellow at the London Center for Policy Research, and a former United States Congressman. A fierce advocate of conservative values, strong education, and public service, Allen West served 22 years in the U.S. Army in several combat zones — including Operation Desert Storm and Operation Iraqi Freedom, achieving the rank of Lt. Colonel.

INTRODUCTION

Harassed. Marginalized. Fined. Incarcerated. Silenced. These adjectives aptly apply not only to the famous group of Pilgrims that set sail on the *Mayflower* in 1620, but to Bible-believing Christians in the United States today. The cultural movements and legal actions taken against the Pilgrims prior to their voyage to America have become eerily similar to those currently taking place in the United States. Like my ancestor William Brewster, Separatist leader and head elder of the Pilgrims, who was fined, jailed, and forced into hiding, Pastors and Christian organizations in modern America are beginning to see difficulties such as these land at their doorsteps.

The Pilgrims have become something of historical folklore, and it is all too easy to forget that this courageous group of men, women, and children seeking religious freedom were real people, facing real persecution, who overcame real odds.

19

Not only did they build the foundation for one of the oldest English settlements in what is now the United States, they also planted the first seed of American democracy by organizing a "civil body politic" governed by the first written framework of government on American soil.[1]

The Pilgrims have a special place in American history, but we have been missing the most important lessons all along. What if we have become a nation that would not only be unwelcoming to these Pilgrims, but one in which they would not seek refuge and religious freedom at all? While almost all children in the United States grow up learning about the Pilgrims at some point during their education, the emphasis on religious freedom and what took place in the years before their voyage to America has all too easily been forgotten. We must remember what took place prior to the Pilgrim's departure for the "New World," how they dealt with a changing culture and increasingly hostile government, who they were before the *Mayflower*, and what they established after arriving at Cape Cod.

This book will set the record straight on the true significance of the Pilgrims in modern-day America. Through exploring who the Pilgrims really were and what they overcame, as well as piecing together the dangerous and hostile actions the United States government and mainstream media have taken towards silencing Christians in America, readers will see the uncanny parallel between what happened to the Pilgrims before their voyage on the *Mayflower* and what is happening in America today.

It is important to note what is meant by "Pilgrims" in regard to whom and what are being analyzed and used for comparison in this book. I am herein referring to the actions taken against, and taken by, the original "Separatists" from the Church of England who first fled to Holland to avoid persecution from King John and the Church of England in the years immediately prior to and following their voyage to America aboard the *Mayflower*. I am not referring to the Puritans, Quakers, or other groups who would eventually join and reorganize the colony, or the participants in the Salem witch trials, which took place more than 70 years and several generations after the founding of Plymouth Colony by the Pilgrims.[2] Rather, this book examines the original inhabitants of Plymouth colony who came aboard the *Mayflower*.

These Pilgrims are the individuals who established Plymouth Colony in 1620 and remained an independent colony before their community was diminished and eclipsed through the reorganization with the Massachusetts Bay Colony, and ultimately immersed into the royal colony of Massachusetts under a new charter in 1691.[3] These are the Pilgrims I am referring to, who did not come for gold, riches, or warfare, but braved the high seas, disease, and starvation in hopes of creating a new life full of religious freedom, honestly obtained private property, and individual liberty. They did not come to the New World to impose their beliefs and oppress others.

The Pilgrims wanted nothing more than to be left alone to live their lives and raise their children according to their beliefs and the Word of God, without hindrance from their government or others.

Certainly, we are not living in the same times and context as the Pilgrims, but if we fail to take away the proper and most important lessons from history, we are destined to repeat it. We must start asking the right questions. Instead of asking what the Pilgrims ate at their first "Thanksgiving feast," or thinking of ways to try and make these historical figures out to be invading hatemongers, we should be asking: what drove the Pilgrims to such great lengths to venture to America, and are these same circumstances occurring again today?

What if Christians have become foreigners in a country founded on Christian principles? What if atheism has become the unofficial, "official" religion of the United States? What if believing in God's Word has moved from being celebrated and welcomed to being demeaned and excluded?

What if I told you that marriage equality has nothing to do with marriage equality? Or that we have become a society that no longer protects and fights for its most innocent and vulnerable, but openly applauds their destruction?

Christians are finding themselves on increasingly marginalized ground in America. While Christians have experienced this before, there are now unprecedented cultural forces and legislative actions being mounted against them in America today. After studying, analyzing, and investigating these actions, one cannot help but wonder what our Pilgrim forefathers would think, and more importantly, do, under these present circumstances.

Would they flee to America, or from it? *Would the Pilgrims still come to America today?*

CHAPTER ONE

P.C.
(Pilgrim Correctness)

The social disease of political correctness has entered daily life, inverting good to bad and attempting to rewrite proud histories as an imposition of white supremacy for which we all should make contrition. ~Robert Agostinelli[4]

In today's ever-sensitive political culture, it seems one can never be too politically correct, or "P.C." The rise of political correctness has obscured reality and hindered the ability to address the real problems at hand, stifling politicians with social straitjackets that leave little room to call things as they see them. One P.C. issue growing in popularity is what I like to call

"Pilgrim Correctness," debating the Pilgrims' actual influence on America. While commemorating the Pilgrims on Thanksgiving is a fun tradition, the Pilgrims actually play an irreplaceable role in the history of America, setting the stage for religious and personal freedoms for centuries to come. Let's set the record straight on the Pilgrims.

The Pilgrim's journey to the New World didn't happen overnight, and in order to understand our situation today, one must understand the Pilgrims before they set sail on the *Mayflower*. Who were these people, really? Were they right-wing, religious nut jobs? Conquering, bloodthirsty Englishmen? In reality, they were simple English men and women who believed that their government and corrupt national church should not play the role of mediator between God and themselves.

In 1534, King Henry VIII established himself as crown of the Church of England, England's new national church, which had previously been a Roman Catholic nation. Those who believed the Church of England was too similar to the Roman Catholic Church wanted simpler, less controlled worship. Consequently, these people became known as "Puritans" because they wanted to purify the church.[5] The Puritans had no intention of separating from the church, which is the clearest distinction between the Puritans and the Pilgrims.[6] The Pilgrim forefathers stem from a different, more "extreme" group known as "Separatists." Deeply convicted that the Church of England was too far gone and too powerful to amend, Separatists sought to form congregations separate from the Church of England.[7]

The Separatists were not exactly living under favorable rule. England's 1559 Act of Uniformity made it illegal to miss a holy day by not attending the official Church of England, fineable by one shilling. Larger fines and incarceration were handed down to those who went as far as to hold an unofficial church service.[8] The Separatist congregation that birthed the Pilgrims operated primarily from Scrooby, Nottinghamshire, England, and by the early 1600s, Separatist leaders were facing heavier persecution from authorities.[9] William Brewster, head Elder of the Separatists, had been fined over $6,000 in today's U.S. dollar for failing to cooperate with the national Church of England and was forced to abandon his position as postmaster.[10]

Facing increased scrutiny, the Separatists fled to Holland, in the Dutch

Netherlands. They were twice apprehended, robbed of their possessions and jailed in the process. Although able to practice their beliefs as they saw fit in Holland, the Separatists encountered a new set of challenges. Leaving the lives they knew behind to live in a foreign country meant acclimating themselves to a new language and culture. After remaining in the city of Leiden for over ten years, the Separatists started to see their children lose their identity as they began to identify more and more with the Dutch. With the congregation only growing older, and the youngest members no longer identifying as English, the Separatists saw themselves facing extinction.[11]

During the Separatists' time in Holland, head elder William Brewster began publishing pamphlets critical of English rule over religion and the state church's intrusion on their beliefs. The pamphlets were smuggled into Scotland in 1619. Once the pamphlets had been traced back to Leiden, English authorities began pressuring the Dutch to extradite Brewster back to England. Brewster managed to evade authorities when an arrest was attempted in September of 1619, and remained in hiding until embarking on the *Mayflower*. His type equipment was seized, and the Netherlands created new regulations on the press that made it illegal to produce pamphlets such as Brewster's. Thomas Brewer, who helped Brewster finance the pamphlets, was apprehended by authorities and later sentenced to fourteen years in prison for his continued role in producing religious publications critical of the government and the Church of England.[12]

The Separatists determined that their best course of action, and last hope, was to leave Holland to establish a new colony in the New World. William Bradford made note of the reasons to pursue this heavily considered plan of action, writing about the "discouragements" the Separatists had in Holland, the hope of discovering "a better, and easier place of living," their young being "drawne away by evill examples into extravagance and dangerous courses," and the "great hope, for the propagating and advancing the gospel of the kingdom of Christ in those remote parts of the world."[13]

This indicates that 1) they believed the hardships of a voyage to America and building a new colony were worth the pursuit of a new home in another foreign land so as to live independently where they could worship under their own conditions, and 2) there was a great fear over the dissolution of their community, congregation, youth, and family unit.[14]

Pastor John Robinson would remain behind with the many who could not make the journey to America at that time, and William Brewster would lead the congregation in America.[15] Initially departing on the *Speedwell*, which had been purchased by the congregation, the Pilgrims met with the *Mayflower*, which was rented by investors to transport additional colonists to help the Pilgrims establish their new colony. Of course the *Speedwell* did not reach America, as it was forced to return to England twice due to leaking. William Bradford alleged that crew members caused the leaking deliberately, but ultimately the *Speedwell* was sold and the group consolidated down to 102 passengers aboard the *Mayflower*, officially setting sail for America on September 6, 1620.[16]

After 66 days at sea, the *Mayflower* reached New England on November 11, 1620, with one passenger and one crew member perishing before arriving at Cape Cod. Originally intending to establish their colony further south, dangerous conditions kept them at bay in Cape Cod. Having surveyed the area for almost a month, on December 16, 1620, the Pilgrims chose an abandoned Wampanoag community in present-day Plymouth, Massachusetts, and began building their colony.[17]

The first months in America proved grueling for the Pilgrims, who combated winter conditions, disease, and starvation. Of the original 102 members who embarked on the *Mayflower*, only 52 remained after the first year in Plymouth. There were originally 17 husband and wife heads of families, but after the first three months, only seven men and three women survived from the 17 pairs.[18]

Four months passed before the Pilgrims made any real contact and communicated with the Pokanoket Wampanoag natives. Remarkably, this contact developed into a peaceful, mutually beneficial relationship. Yes, it is true that the Pilgrims had an earlier, unpleasant encounter with the natives, one encounter that is, during the initial landing party. According to William Bradford's narrative, "arrows came flying" and "one lustie man, and no less valiente, was seen shoot 3 arrowes."[19] The landing party returned fire (returned fire, not initiated) as the natives fled. No casualties or injuries were suffered by either party during the skirmish, as the conflict was nothing more than both groups acting out of self-defense.

The Pokanoket Wampanoag had previous, unfriendly encounters with white Europeans, and acted on what little they knew about the Pilgrims: the assumption that they were there to bring them harm. After the Pokanoket Wampanoag started shooting arrows at the landing party, the colonists returned fire. Who wouldn't in that circumstance, as a sitting duck for incoming arrows? No harm was done that day, and the Pilgrims never took or forced the Pokanoket Wampanoag off their land. The Pilgrims settled on a plot of land that had been abandoned and was not wanted by the Pokanoket Wampanoag.

Relief from the Pilgrims' struggles and probable demise came from a native named Squanto, who taught the Pilgrims the necessary hunting, fishing, and farming skills to survive. The Pilgrims believed Squanto, who previously had lived in London after being captured by English sailors, to be the divine providence of God. After all the Pilgrims had been through, it isn't hard to imagine why.[20]

The early struggles and anguish suffered by the Pilgrims turned to a plentiful harvest the following fall, with the help from Squanto and other native Pokanoket Wampanoag. Overcoming demoralizing sickness, death, and the everyday struggle to survive, the Pilgrims marked their successful harvest with a feast, celebration, and thanksgiving to God, which lasted three days.

William Brewster led the Pilgrims in a thanksgiving prayer, and nearly one-hundred Pokanoket Wampanoag men, led by Chief Massasoit, joined with the Pilgrims.[21] Imagine that- two vastly different groups of people, from different backgrounds, cultures, ideas, and beliefs, coming together in unison to celebrate something bigger than themselves. No practices or beliefs were forced on either group that day. Rather, they simply accepted and celebrated their different traditions without impeding on one another, with each party being free to practice their beliefs as they chose. During the coming years, more English colonists joined the colony, including many who had remained in Holland, and by 1627, approximately 160 people lived comfortably in Plymouth Colony.[22]

Two significant events within the story of the Pilgrims, each covenants in their own respect, deserve more attention than they receive. The first is the Mayflower Compact. Drafted and signed upon arriving at Cape Cod on November 11, 1620, the Mayflower Compact was drafted in response to the colonists' arrival with an expired patent from their investors. Colonists who took the voyage on the *Mayflower*, who were not affiliated with the Separatist congregation, sought to take advantage of the situation by doing as they chose, disregarding the contract they made with investors who helped fund the voyage in exchange for commodities from the colony.

As William Bradford wrote, there were "discontented and mutinous speeches" being made by passengers of the *Mayflower* who had accompanied the Pilgrims.[23] Seeking to maintain order while establishing some sense of social unity and disbanding the civic unrest, the Pilgrims produced the first governing document of their colony, and the first of its kind on American soil.

Arranging themselves into a "civil body politic," all issues regarding the colony would be solved democratically by voting under majority rule, including the Mayflower Compact itself. Of the 73 male passengers aboard the *Mayflower*, 41 male

Pilgrims signed and ratified the document. A written democracy was thereby created and ratified for Plymouth Colony, an unprecedented event at the time. While the original document has been lost, there are three surviving versions from the 17th century, including a hand written copy from William Bradford's journal dated 1646.[24] The modern translation reads as follows:

> In the name of God, Amen. We, whose names are underwritten, the loyal subjects of our dread Sovereign Lord King James, by the Grace of God, of Great Britain, France, and Ireland, King, defender of the Faith, etc.
>
> Having undertaken, for the Glory of God, and advancements of the Christian faith and honor of our King and Country, a voyage to plant the first colony in the Northern parts of Virginia, do by these presents, solemnly and mutually, in the presence of God, and one another, covenant and combine ourselves together into a civil body politic; for our better ordering, and preservation and furtherance of the ends aforesaid; and by virtue hereof to enact, constitute, and frame, such

just and equal laws, ordinances, acts, constitutions, and offices, from time to time, as shall be thought most meet and convenient for the general good of the colony; unto which we promise all due submission and obedience.

In witness whereof we have hereunto subscribed our names at Cape Cod the 11th of November, in the year of the reign of our Sovereign Lord King James, of England, France, and Ireland, the eighteenth, and of Scotland, the fifty-fourth, 1620.[25]

Thus the Pilgrims embedded clear traces of democratic inclinations in the Mayflower Compact. Their reasoning and objectives also come to light in this compact, which shows the dual nature of their intentions. First, the Pilgrims sought to obtain a level of independence which granted them the liberty to live freely and unrestrained according to their beliefs, and second, to simultaneously preserve their ties to England.[26]

The Pilgrims knew the immense value of freedom of religion, speech, conscience, thought, and press because they lived through the harassment and oppression of governing authorities trying to restrict them. Equally important was their understanding of God's law, including their respect for others, which they demonstrated by not imposing their beliefs on non-Separatists. Pilgrim men were the majority on the *Mayflower*, and they could have established a Theocracy or required every non-Separatist colonist or Native American near Plymouth Colony to accept their beliefs or suffer restrictions. But they didn't. Instead, they chose to live peacefully according to their beliefs, in a democratic framework, genuinely centered on the general welfare of the colony, without imposing their beliefs on anyone or restricting others from practicing theirs.

These same admirable qualities were demonstrated by Chief Massasoit and the Pokanoket Wampanoag tribe, who not only learned to co-exist with the Pilgrims, but saw to their survival and well-being. This was achieved through a second significant covenant within the story of the Pilgrims: the treaty between the Pilgrims and Chief Massasoit, initiated by Chief Massasoit himself, established in March of 1621.[27] This treaty signifies not only the special relationship between these two groups and their ability to live side-by-side, but also their mutual respect, gratitude, tolerance, and equality. How many other white

Europeans would have invited Native Americans as honored guests to a three day celebration in the 1600s?

Given the poor relationship between white Europeans and Native Americans at this time, and the negative encounters Chief Massasoit and Squanto had experienced, it is truly astonishing that the treaty is known as a treaty of mutual *protection*, not simply mutual *do-no-harm*. While the treaty did establish that they would bring no harm to the other, it also established that they would aid each other in times of war. The treaty contained the following elements:

> 1) Neither party will harm the other
> 2) If any property is stolen it is to be returned, and the offending person sent to his own people to be reprimanded
> 3) Neither party will bring weapons when meeting
> 4) The two parties will aid each other as allies in times of war[28]

The treaty was successfully upheld and points to the true character of Chief Massasoit and our Pilgrim forefathers, who continued to survive and thrive alongside one another, all while respecting their vastly different cultures and beliefs. These models of tolerance embodied who the Pilgrims really were, and demonstrates why their story, 150 years prior to the American Revolution, remains such a compelling and matchless piece of American history.

The Pilgrims rightfully earned a place in history textbooks, but more importantly, the right to be remembered for who they really were and what they overcame before they ever stepped foot on the *Mayflower*. Yes, we must remember the Pilgrims for who they really were, not as the overtly caricaturized people tied to Puritans because their story revolves around religion and religious liberty. There is no need to try and prove the worth of the Pilgrims and their impact on American history; it's written in the underlying themes and freedoms that helped shape America. It is, however, necessary to study and learn from the courageous actions of these individuals, rather than simply the broad trends and movements of that time period.[29]

An unprecedented celebration in Plymouth, Massachusetts in 1920, marking the three hundred year anniversary of the Pilgrim's landing at Plymouth Rock, did just that. The event featured speakers including U.S. President Warren Harding, the Massachusetts governor, Senator Henry Cabot Lodge, and Dutch and British ambassadors. A crowd so large was generated that it was said to have caused a traffic jam that was "the worst ever in Southeastern Massachusetts."[30]

Senator Lodge, a Republican and historian from Massachusetts who is credited as being the first U.S. Senate Majority Leader, delivered a commemoration speech at this event that is worthy of further examination today. Senator Lodge describes the Pilgrim's landing at Plymouth Rock as a decisive event that had "something of world effect," stating that the Pilgrim's achievement was something not to be taken for granted:

> Following the migrations of the Mayflower descendants and of the children of New England across the continent, until now in ever-increasing numbers the anniversary of the landing in 1620 is marked and celebrated with each recurring year from the Atlantic to the Pacific. The deeds of the little band of hunted men and women have come into their own.[31]

Indeed they have. But one must wonder if all of the focus on turkey, football and the misbranding of the Puritans and Pilgrims in to one big misconception has eclipsed what the 102 passengers on the *Mayflower* accomplished, and has blinded us from seeing the Pilgrim's story before they landed at Plymouth Rock being re-written in our own country today.

To Senator Lodge, the Pilgrims exemplified self-control, and in its own sense, a form of liberty, because "the right of man to private property honestly obtained was essential to social stability and to civilization." Senator Lodge stated that while the Puritans "resisted for half a century the inevitable result with all the fierce energy of earnest men strong both in character and in intellect, and failed," the Pilgrims "opened the door to the coming of freedom of conscience, and freedom of conscience meant freedom of thought," and consequently, "they succeeded marvelously."[32]

The Pilgrims were not perfect people, but like it or not, the Pilgrims embody what makes America, America. Now is the time when *our* America must hold itself up to a mirror, and ask whether or not our country has morphed into a land in which the Pilgrims would no longer be welcomed. The Pilgrims represent far too great a triumph, too great an ideal, too great an example of freedom of conscience and thought, and too much of what made America the country it became to be whisked away so effortlessly by typecasts, false pretenses, misconceptions, and forgetfulness. The Pilgrims' story is one that not only carries great historical significance, but relevance that has transcended time, race, color, age, and the advancement of the United States. Its relevance, however, has never been more important in America than it is today. Without proper understanding of where the Pilgrims once were, who they were, and where they ended up, we will see the dark side of history repeat itself once more.

In this crash-course in Pilgrim Correctness, what have we learned? Where are we at now? Let's fast-forward almost exactly 396 years from the attempted arrest of William Brewster in 1619 to present-day America, the shining beacon of freedom and liberty. What we find is that government authorities in Houston, the fifth largest city in America, issued subpoenas to five pastors, demanding that all sermons, notes, and communications be turned over to the office of the openly lesbian and liberal-progressive mayor, Annise Parker, for censorship.[33] Why? Because the pastors were part of a group that was critical of new government legislation that would allow full-grown men who say they identify as women to waltz in to any women's restroom at any time. How far we have come!

Essentially, government authorities targeted and bullied pastors into handing over their sermons because they were critical of laws infringing on religious liberty and their congregations' beliefs, and attempted to seize sermons, notes, and communications from pastors who were attempting to influence their congregation to oppose the government's new legislation. Sound familiar? This is not an isolated incident, nor the only circumstance in which we have seen our government come down on pastors and Christians in America. Perhaps Christians living in the United States today have more in common with, and more to learn from, the Pilgrims than just an annual Thanksgiving celebration.

CHAPTER TWO

The Modern Day Pilgrim

"If we lose our freedom here, where do we go?"
~Pastor Rafael Cruz

The dictionary provides a simple, straightforward definition for the word "pilgrim."

1. a person who journeys, especially a long distance, to some sacred place as an act of religious devotion:

2. a traveler or wanderer, especially in a foreign place.[34]

However, like many things, it takes a second glance to fully appreciate and understand what's there. What makes a "pilgrim" a "pilgrim"? The above definition certainly describes the group of Separatists who established Plymouth Colony, but this definition is beginning to take on a whole new meaning with people in America today who had never given it a second thought: Christians.

America is not a Christian nation- it is a free nation founded on Christian principles. These principles, such as faith, family, liberty, and freedom, are being replaced by bigger, more intrusive government, relative truths, and "progress" that divides the American people by any means possible.

America today is not the America the Founding Fathers knew or envisioned, nor is it the country it was even 50 years ago. For Christians, America is no longer the country that welcomes, celebrates, or even tolerates their faith. Our country has turned to one with an increasingly hostile attitude towards Christianity and a shrinking tolerance for those who choose to follow God and their most deeply held beliefs in accordance with the Bible. What is happening in America is not what is happening in the Middle East and other regions of the world, where

Christians face extreme persecution and death, but when our culture openly dismisses Christians and our government continues to stand in opposition to the Church, clearly Christians in America are not living in the country they once knew.

What if Christians in America have become foreigners in their own country? Impossible, some might say, as there are many churches and Christians in America; we are, after all, a free nation. When we start to look at what is happening in our nation, however, Christians in America are residing in what is becoming a foreign place, embodying the very definition of a "pilgrim."

Consider the following remarks from Rev. E.W. Jackson, speaking to over 600 pastors at the Family Research Council's "Watchmen on the Wall" event on May 22, 2015 in Washington D.C.:[35]

> It bothers me to think my own country is a strange land. I never thought there would be a day when my nation would persecute the Bible-believing Christian for standing for what the word of God says and reward those who come against it as if they are heroes; as if they are great Americans for

standing up against God, but that's where we are.

I never thought that I would see the day when people would brag about their ability to destroy children in the womb, but that's exactly what we have today, and not only brag about it, but demand that your taxpayer dollars go to support the destruction of unborn children.

It ought to make us weep. Sometimes it seems like we're living in a foreign land.[36]

These remarks hit the nail on the head and further demonstrate the key point here: Christians in America have become pilgrims in their own country.

So how did we get here? What has led to the increasingly hostile attitude towards Christianity in America? To put it plainly, liberal, socially progressive policies that seek to undermine religion and dismiss Christianity and its role in America are putting the church at odds with the government. The mainstream media continues to praise those who come against God and the Bible, while shaming and ignoring those who stand for what they believe in.

For example, it's no coincidence that Tim Tebow, one of the most outspoken professing Christian in sports, was also the most scrutinized and loathed athlete in America. Even though he built a hospital in the Philippines and proved to be a better role model than perhaps any other player in the NFL, and is someone who children should actually look up to, he was constantly told to keep his religion and beliefs–the driving force behind who he is as a person–to himself. ESPN, the rest of the media, and most of America wanted nothing to do with what makes Tim Tebow who he is and what he believes in. However, when gay athletes come out, they are hailed as heroes for standing up and talking about what makes them who they are and what they believe.

Tim Tebow certainly isn't an isolated example of the media shunning and ostracizing Christians. When Phil Robertson of the television show *Duck Dynasty,* an extremely popular show based around a strong Christian family that was reaching millions of people and growing in popularity and influence, made "controversial" comments about homosexuality (he was well known before the controversy as a Bible-believing Christian who believes marriage is between one man and one woman, who was asked by a reporter his views on homosexuality), liberal media and political commentators were armed and ready to heap down fire and brimstone on the heads of the Robertson family to ensure that the show would get pulled from the air.

Take NFL Quarterback Robert Griffin for another example, who was told to turn his t-shirt that read "Know Jesus Know Peace/ No Jesus No Peace" inside out before beginning a post-game press conference. The t-shirt was unmistakably a Christian message reflecting his personal beliefs, and while some reporters were quick to point out that it is the policy of the NFL that only official Nike gear be worn by players during a press conference, there were other players at the same press conference wearing non-Nike gear while talking to reporters at the press conference who were not told to turn their shirts inside out.[37] With all of the problems the NFL has had recently with player arrests for DUI's, domestic violence, and child abuse among others, maybe a message like the one Robert Griffin tried to portray that day is one the NFL should start welcoming.

It is evident that American culture today does not accept, appreciate, welcome, or even tolerate Christians today the way it once did. While culture has shifted dramatically, surely our elected leader, President Obama, who says he identifies as Christian, and got enough votes from Christians in 2008 and 2012 to become President, would right the ship and stand up for Christians, churches, and Christian values. These are some of his sentiments on Christianity:

> Unless we get on our high horse and think this is unique to some other place, remember that during the Crusades and the Inquisition, people committed terrible deeds in the name of Christ. In our home country, slavery and Jim Crow all too often was justified in the name of Christ.[38]

This quote from President Obama himself, speaking at the 2015 National Prayer Breakfast of all places, where he chose to call on Christians to get off of their high horse because of terrible deeds done by Christians some thousand years ago during the Crusades, and because of slavery and Jim Crow in America. Perhaps someone should remind President Obama that Christians were at the forefront of the fight to abolish slavery, and then ask him which party it was who fought to end slavery.

But undoubtedly the President must have gotten it right on Easter, of all days. Speaking at the White House on Easter of 2015, to a room full of pastors, cardinals, ministers, and other people of faith, the President said, "On Easter, I do reflect on the fact that as a Christian, I am supposed to love, and I have to say that sometimes when I listen to less-than-loving expressions by Christians, I get concerned. But that's a topic for another day. I was about to veer off, I'm pulling it back."[39]

Just when you thought President Obama couldn't do more damage! Another zinger aimed directly at Christians, on Easter, just four days after he refused to make any reference of religion when discussing the savage, targeted massacre of Christians at the hands of Islamic extremists in Kenya.[40]

We'll let the President off the hook (momentarily), since, after all, America is currently a very politically divided nation, split almost down the middle. However, it is undeniable that it is liberal, socially progressive policies and ideology that are punishing Christians in America. You don't have to be a political commentator or political science professor to notice that the policies, ideas, and attacks that undermine Churches and individual religious liberty come from one side: the liberal left, while it is the conservatives who are fighting to protect religious institutions and freedoms.

It was liberal Democrats in California who voted to remove the words "husband" and "wife" from California laws, and now want to do so at the federal level (in response to the Supreme Court's decision to redefine marriage), because the traditional terms are too "oppressive." You can't make this stuff up. Liberal law makers in California passed a bill that was signed into law by Gov. Jerry Brown in July, 2014, that eliminated the words "husband" and "wife" from California's marriage law.[41] This is the kind of dangerous, liberal agenda and ideology that undermines Christians, their beliefs, and the family unit that has served as the cornerstone of Western Civilization.

I know multiple families who have left California, often considered the most liberal state in the Union, to escape the rampant corruption, moral decay, and cultural disaster that has taken place there. Picture that: Americans packing up and leaving their homes in search of a better life in another region of their own country, because there is nowhere else to go. Meanwhile, conservatives are fighting on behalf of Christians to ensure that the government ceases to intrude on individual religious freedom. How far we have come from the days when liberals also championed religious liberty. In 1993, President Bill Clinton signed the Religious Freedom Restoration Act into law, after it moved through the House of Representatives unanimously, and passed through the Senate on a 97-3 vote.

Ironically, this federal law accomplished the same thing that caused a national outcry in March and April of 2015, when Indiana adopted a RFRA, which was ultimately amended.[42] But you won't hear Hillary or Bill Clinton touting this fact today, as the liberal agenda continues to come down on Churches and conservative groups and non-profits. This is simply another clear indication of the way things are shifting: further and further away from anything that has to do with Christianity.

Something dangerous has happened in our country, particularly among the mainstream media, that has spread like wildfire: the idea that we have suddenly become above God. The notion that the human race has evolved and advanced so far that we are now smarter and more capable than ever, and therefore we no longer need God. When did America become too good for God? The media loves to portray anyone who believes in the Bible as small-minded, irrational, hateful, and incapable of reason.

Here's something liberal talk-show hosts, politicians, and every other person who claims Christians are ignorant or senseless should be reminded of: Martin Luther King Jr. wasn't just Martin Luther King Jr.–he was *Reverend* Martin Luther King Jr. People love to leave out that word in front of his name. Not only was he a devout Christian, he was a pastor and leader of an entire congregation.

What about William Wilberforce, leader of the abolition movement in England, and Corrie ten Boom, who helped save and hide Jews during the Nazi Holocaust? Were they close-minded bigots for believing in the word of God? How about Mother Theresa, Jackie Robinson, and Abraham Lincoln? Were they all incompetent, silly Christians for believing in the Bible? The list goes on and on. Chances are, if George Washington, the Father of America, wasn't above the Bible, then neither are we. Someone should be asking Bill Maher why he called Rev. Martin Luther King Jr., William Wilberforce, Corrie ten Boom, Mother Theresa, Abraham Lincoln, Jackie Robinson, and many other American heroes stupid, since after all, according to Bill, anyone who believes in the Bible is stupid.[43]

People like to throw around statistics such as "70 percent of Americans are Christians." Really? If 70 percent of Americans were true, Bible-believing Christians, church attendance among Americans wouldn't be at less than 20 percent, and several thousand churches wouldn't be closing their doors each year.[44] Abortion would never have been legalized, let alone funded with tax dollars; marriage would still be structured the way God intended; 50 percent of marriages wouldn't be ending in divorce; Planned Parenthood clinics would be replaced with adoption agencies and actual women's health clinics; Christian schools and non-profits wouldn't be in danger of losing accreditation and tax-exempt status; pastors wouldn't be facing fines and jail time; and the government wouldn't be pitting itself against churches.

It's easy to think that everything is sunshine and rainbows for Christians in America, but the next time someone tries to tell you that Christians have it better off than anyone else, show them this book, especially the next chapter, where the marginalization, harassment, and oppression of Christians in America will be laid out in more detail.

Yes, the story of the Pilgrims is a great tale that has turned in to legend, but while Christians and conservatives may be the most likely to identify with and study the story of the Pilgrims, it's our liberal friends who should appreciate what the Pilgrims accomplished the most.

You see, the Pilgrim forefathers who founded Plymouth Colony helped establish separation of church and state and chose to stand up to a national church that was burdening, harassing, and persecuting those who did not follow the strict orders of the Church of England. They essentially were living under theocratic rule in England under King John, but the Pilgrims elected to fight the oppressive national church, leading the way to a New World where individuals were free to worship or *not* worship as they so chose.

However, while the Pilgrims were fleeing a tyrannical, repressive, corrupt national church, Christians in America today find themselves at odds not only with the culture and media, but also with the very government that established a democratic framework built on protecting religious liberty.

America has accomplished and established too much and Christianity has come too far in helping develop the greatest country in the history of the world to let it all slip away now. People have to wake up and start paying attention. We need to hold our elected officials accountable.

In 2008 we elected a President who, as a state senator in Illinois, openly and proudly voted against a bill that would have protected babies who survived late term abortions. He took issue with the part of the bill that stated, "A live child born as a result of an abortion shall be fully recognized as a human person and accorded immediate protection under the law."[45] The vote he cast meant he believes that any child who survives an abortion still deserves to die. I'll repeat: as a state senator, President Obama voted to deny the protection of life and basic human rights to babies who survive an abortion and are born alive. Where was the media coverage on that extreme position?

Ready for a gut check? The greatest freedom in America isn't freedom to choose among religions, but rather, it's the freedom to choose or *not* choose any religion. People living in England during the 1500-1600s were forced to follow the teachings of the corrupt Church of England and it destroyed people's lives. In America, we know everyone has the freedom to follow or not follow God. That's what makes America so great, and it's what the Pilgrim's helped establish: the ability to choose to follow or not follow God as you determine best. The problem today, however, is that the ability to not choose God has overpowered the ability to choose God, and not choosing God is now not only favorable, but those who do choose to follow God are being marginalized and ostracized to the point that Christians are becoming outcasts in a country founded on Christian principles.

"God bless America:" these three words are used at the end of practically every speech given by the President of the United States. This includes President Barack Obama–the same President Obama who chose to criticize Christians on the National Day of Prayer and on Easter in the midst of recent, barbaric attacks on Christians in the Middle East, and who believes babies who survive abortions should be denied basic human rights.

Every time a tragedy occurs and people are angry, suffering, and hurting, leaders will attend and lead prayer vigils and deliver powerful speeches, talking about prayer and looking and reaching out to God, and of course, ending with "God bless America."

God bless America? Why would He? As our country continues to remove any and all references to God or Christianity from schools, public buildings, and culture, while thousands and thousands of babies, His children, are being led to the slaughter every year? God bless America? While we have ignored everything the Bible says about marriage to make it what modern man wants it to be? America has turned its back on God. We don't have to follow God; that is every individual's choice. But when those who do are turned into outcasts and

Christianity is completely disregarded by our society, government, and culture, there's no reason for God to bless America. Perhaps, instead, we should be saying, "God have mercy on America."

The First Amendment is under attack in America, and we know this. This should not only be concerning to the most sincere Christians in America, but to everyone. The First Amendment is the First Amendment for a reason; if we lose the aspect of freedom of religion embedded in the First Amendment, what happens to freedom of speech? If you're not allowed to talk about or practice your religion, you no longer have freedom of speech. When you lose the First Amendment, you also lose freedom of press, as you can no longer print religious pamphlets. When you lose the First Amendment, you lose the right to petition your government, because you can no longer petition your government over religion.

The list goes on, and suddenly this all looks awfully familiar to our Pilgrim forefathers, such as William Brewster, who did lose these freedoms as the government encroached further and further on their freedoms and religious beliefs. When this happened, the Pilgrims sought refuge in the Netherlands, and when they ran out of time there, they fled to the New World and established their own colony. If we do lose our freedoms here, where will people go? America is no longer the safe harbor for Christianity that it once was. It is not like Iraq, Iran, or Afghanistan, but America is no longer laying out the welcoming mat for Christians. The story of the Pilgrims has never been more relevant than it is today, especially for Christians in America. The difference, however, is that now there may be nowhere left to go.

CHAPTER THREE

Atheism: Official Religion of the United States of America

"Of all the dispositions and habits which lead to political prosperity, religion and morality are indispensable." ~ George Washington

When the Pilgrims arrived in the New World and founded Plymouth Colony, they had a decision to make: how would they govern themselves for the betterment of the colony? We know that the Pilgrims fled England in pursuit of religious freedom and built their own colony, in which they had the power to create a theocracy, but they didn't. Instead, they established a civil body politic reliant on democracy and freedom of religion.

This is similar, of course, to what the Founding Fathers ultimately constructed in America. America is not a Christian nation; it was never intended to be one, and never has been one. Although Christianity is not the "official" religion of the United States, no one ever dreamt that it would begin to be marginalized the way it is today.

We must begin to ask ourselves, what happens when atheism and religious *intolerance* become the unofficial, "official" position of the United States?

The United States government is never supposed to enforce a state religion, but when the government begins persecuting Christianity in order not only to not favor it, but to support the dissolution of the Christian faith by backing atheism and demonstrating religious intolerance, what exactly are they doing? Just because atheism is the concept that there is no God doesn't mean it's not a belief. It's exactly that: the belief that there is nothing more, and this belief produces the dangerous ideology that truth is merely relative.

The religious intolerance we are seeing is unprecedented on American soil. It's time Americans start waking up to the harsh reality that Christians who actually want to live out their faith on a daily basis are unwelcome to do so. All one has to do is look at the increasingly hostile actions the United States government has been taking against religion, along with the cultural trends that move further and further away from anything that has to do with Christianity, and it can easily be seen that Christians have lost their place in America.

The bigger government gets, the smaller individual freedom becomes. The United States government is bigger today than it has ever been, and it's no coincidence that religious freedom is also in more danger than it's ever been. Outlined on the following pages are just some of the recent examples that demonstrate the growing religious intolerance in America, and what Christians are now up against.

- ❖ Houston Mayor Annise Parker generated and issued subpoenas for five Houston pastors, demanding that all sermons and material dealing with homosexuality and gender identity be turned over to her office for censorship.[46]

- ❖ City officials in Idaho created ordinances that threatened pastors with fines and jail time for their refusal to marry homosexuals.[47]

- ❖ In Kentucky, Chaplain David Wells was forced to choose between signing a document vowing that he would stop preaching homosexuality was a sin, or be stripped of his credentials as an ordained minister by the Kentucky Department of Juvenile Justice. He refused to sign the document and his credentials were revoked, putting an end to Chaplain Wells' work with underage inmates at the Warren County Regional Juvenile Detention Center, to whom he ministered for 13 years.[48]

❖ Christian-based businesses and organizations such as Hobby Lobby and Colorado Christian University, among others, needed to fight all the way to the U.S. Supreme Court in order to not be forced to pay for their employees to have abortions provided in their health care plan.[49]

❖ Jack Phillips, owner of a cake shop in Lakewood, Colorado, was sued by a homosexual couple for not participating in their wedding due to his religious beliefs. A Colorado judge ruled in favor of the homosexual couple.[50]

❖ A school in Montgomery County, Maryland removed all references to religious holidays from its school calendar.[51]

❖ A Federal Appeals Court in Denver, Colorado, ruled against Little Sisters of the Poor (a group of nuns dedicated to serving the elderly) in a contraception coverage case, effectively forcing the nuns to choose between their faith and their work helping the poor and elderly.[52]

❖ Christian bakers in Oregon were fined $135,000 for refusing to make a wedding cake for a lesbian couple.[53]

❖ In Columbia, Missouri, the Boone County Commission voted to remove an Operation Desert Storm Memorial from the county courthouse due to an engraving of a "Jesus Fish" on the memorial.[54]

❖ Under the Obama administration the IRS targeted and subjected conservative Christian groups to intensive scrutiny over tax exempt status and other issues (you can bet Churches will be next).[55]

❖ The Obama Administration openly admitted that the tax-exempt status of universities and churches who oppose same-sex marriage are now at risk and will "be an issue" during the U.S. Supreme Court gay marriage case Obergefell v. Hodges.[56] Consequently, Christian schools and non-profits are now in danger of losing accreditation and tax exempt status after the Supreme Court ruled to redefine marriage and make gay marriage the law of the land.

There can now be no question that the culture in America today wants nothing to do with Christianity. Many more instances could be added here, as the list goes on and on, as prayer and any references to the Bible are being taken out of schools, and any reference to God or religion in the public square is under constant threat of being removed.[57]

In fact, the list is so much longer and comprehensive that the Liberty Institute and Family Research Council created a 367 page report titled "Undeniable: The Survey of Hostility to Religion in America," which documents the growing cases of anti-Christian persecution in America.[58] The report lists and describes hundreds of cases where religious liberty has been denied or where people have been persecuted for their Christian beliefs.

Take a look at just a few of the cases outlined in this report:

❖ A federal judge threatened "incarceration" to a high school valedictorian unless she removed references to Jesus from her graduation speech.[59]

❖ City officials prohibited senior citizens from praying over their meals, listening to religious messages, or singing gospel songs at a senior activities center.[60]

❖ A public school official physically lifted an elementary school student

from his seat and reprimanded him
in front of his classmates for praying
over his lunch.[61]

❖ Following U.S. Department of
Veterans Affairs' policies, a federal
government official sought to censor
a pastor's prayer, eliminating
references to Jesus, during a
Memorial Day ceremony honoring
veterans at a national cemetery.[62]

❖ Public school officials prohibited
students from handing out gifts
because they contained religious
messages.[63]

❖ A public school official prevented a
student from handing out flyers
inviting her classmates to an event
at her church.[64]

❖ A public university's law school
banned a Christian organization
because it required its officers to
adhere to a statement of faith that
the university disagreed with.[65]

- ❖ The U.S. Department of Justice argued before the Supreme Court that the federal government can tell churches and synagogues which pastors and rabbis it can hire and fire.[66]

- ❖ Through the Patient Protection and Affordable Care Act, also known as Obamacare, the federal government is forcing religious organizations to provide insurance for birth control and abortion inducing drugs in direct violation of their religious beliefs.[67]

- ❖ The U.S. Department of Veterans Affairs banned the mention of God from veterans' funerals, overriding the wishes of the deceased veterans' families.[68]

Speaking on the sharp increase in cases involving hostility towards Christians in America, Liberty Institute founder Kelly Shackleford stated:

It is dramatic. I have been doing these types of cases for almost 25 years now. I have never seen the levels of attacks like these and how quickly they are now proliferating. There are children being prohibited from writing Merry Christmas to the soldiers, senior citizens being banned from praying over their meals in the Senior Center, the VA banning the mention of God in military funerals, numerous attempts to have veteran's memorials torn down if they have any religious symbols such as a cross, and I could go on and on.[69]

Modern America is not close to anything the Pilgrims or Founding Fathers ever could have envisioned as a land where people could openly practice their faith and raise their children. Things may look rosy for Christians on Sunday mornings, but when in the history of our country has there ever been as much backlash towards religion as we see today? Maybe the Pilgrims and our Founding Fathers knew something that I fear many today have long forgotten. They understood that there is no greater freedom than religious freedom, and they went to great lengths to achieve it. It seems that today's culture is going to great lengths to destroy it.[70]

While hundreds of years have passed since the Pilgrims first landed at Plymouth Rock and the Founding Fathers wrote the United States Constitution, shouldn't the fact that the most famous and historical figures in American history wouldn't even recognize the land they once called home serve as a wake-up call for all Americans?

I will reiterate the point that no one is required to be Christian to be an American, nor should they have to be, but one thing has become evidently clear in recent years and is the trajectory of years to come: Christians have lost their place in America. Not only have they lost their place, but they are being marginalized to the point where it seems safest for Christians to just stay in their homes, keep quiet, and conform to the world around them whenever they step outside.

If you know your history, and your "Pilgrim Correctness," you know that the Separatists went through something similar to what we are seeing today in America, and that they experienced this in England and the Netherlands before the term "Pilgrim" was ever coined or the voyage on the *Mayflower* ever took place. Their culture and government wanted nothing to do with them. They became outcasts and radicals; new laws were created that more and more infringed on their most deeply held beliefs, and eventually they were effectively driven out of their own country.

The real issue, however, is not just when culture and government want nothing to do with Christians, it's when they are no longer content with simply ignoring Christians and letting believers practice their faith privately, but decide they must go a step further and diminish, marginalize, harass, and silence Christians.

This is what we are beginning to see today in America, and this is truly a sad time for our country. Things were not always so bleak, as not so long ago the Pilgrims and Founding Fathers were celebrated properly, as was their faith in God, as heroes with virtue for all of America to admire.

In fact, it is well known that the Pilgrims play a major role in the United

States Capitol building's Rotunda. Featured in the Rotunda are: the *Landing of the Pilgrims*, completed in 1825 (one of four reliefs resting over the Rotunda doors), a painting of the *Embarkation of the Pilgrims at Delft Haven, Holland, July 22nd, 1620*, completed in 1843 (one of eight large paintings in the Rotunda), and the scene of *the Landing of Pilgrims at Plymouth, Mass., 1620* which lies within the Rotunda frieze.[71]

Lesser known, however, is the emblematic painting of William Brewster, which is located in the President's room of the Senate Wing in the United States Capitol. The painting of William Brewster was made to represent religion, as one of four symbolic paintings in the President's room.[72] The other three paintings include Christopher Columbus (signifying discovery), Benjamin Franklin (signifying history), and Americus Vespucius (signifying exploration).

The point here is simple: the Pilgrims play a crucial role in American history, and yet the remembrance and most important lessons from the Pilgrims have been pushed aside. It is not hard to imagine that if the United States Capitol building were to be demolished and rebuilt today, the various depictions of the Pilgrims in the Rotunda may be left out–the painting of

William Brewster signifying religion in the President's room certainly would be.

Who and what would replace the themes of William Brewster and religion, Christopher Columbus and discovery, Benjamin Franklin and history, and Americus Vespucius and exploration in the President's Room today?

Toss out William Brewster and religion, and replace it with evolution and a portrait of Charles Darwin. Get rid of Christopher Columbus and discovery, and exchange it for a picture of Caitlyn Jenner to symbolize courage. Take down Benjamin Franklin and history, and put up Margaret Sanger for reproductive rights. Tear down Americus Vespucius and exploration, and hoist up Hillary Clinton signifying fairness. There's your new President's room in present day America.

In America today, you can be anyone you want to be. Heck, we'll even let you pick your own race and gender. Just don't offend anyone with your Christian beliefs, you know, the same ones that helped start America–the same ones that were held by George Washington, Martin Luther King Jr., and Jackie Robinson. It appears in America today anyone really can be whatever they choose and can identify with anything, but if

you choose Christianity, you'll find yourself
on unwelcoming ground.

CHAPTER FOUR

The Spectrum of Welcome

"I expect to die in bed, my successor will die in prison and his successor will die a martyr in the public square." ~ Chicago Cardinal Francis George

Is it really possible that Christians have not only lost their place in America, but are no longer welcome here? Critics will say this is impossible, citing the misleading notion that "70 percent of Americans are Christian" and that there are multitudes of churches. If you're paying attention to what is happening in America today and remember what happened to the Pilgrims during their time in England and the Netherlands, the similarities become self-evident as both groups reached a certain point of hostility from their homelands.

It is important to understand what being "welcome" and "unwelcome" actually mean. When I say Christians are living on increasingly unwelcoming ground in America, that doesn't mean they aren't allowed to live here anymore or are being persecuted to the point of death. It does mean, however, that Christians in America are moving the wrong direction on the "Spectrum of Welcome."

Visuals are always helpful, and things aren't always opposite extremes such as being welcome or unwelcome, which is why the "Spectrum of Welcome" chart was created- to show the different stages of welcoming. The following charts showing the "Spectrum of Welcome" will help put in to perspective where Christians in America are at today, where they have been, and where they are going.

SPECTRUM of WELCOME

The "Spectrum of Welcome"[73] is the idea of Jeannie Edwards of Centennial Institute, and was translated into a chart by the author.

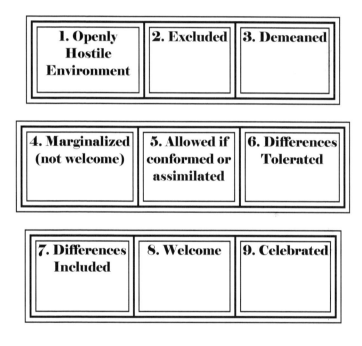

| 1. Openly Hostile Environment | 2. Excluded | 3. Demeaned |

| 4. Marginalized (not welcome) | 5. Allowed if conformed or assimilated | 6. Differences Tolerated |

| 7. Differences Included | 8. Welcome | 9. Celebrated |

There are nine stages in the "Spectrum of Welcome" demonstrating the different levels of welcoming a group can receive. This helps people visualize the actual place a certain group of people have within the larger whole. As this chart demonstrates, just because one is not in an openly hostile environment, does not mean they are entirely welcome, or for that matter, even tolerated.

Spectrum of Welcome: Pilgrims in England Prior to Fleeing to the Netherlands

1. Openly Hostile Environment	2. Excluded	3. Demeaned

4. Marginalized (not welcome)	5. Allowed if conformed or assimilated	6. Differences Tolerated

7. Differences Included	8. Welcome	9. Celebrated

The only reason the Pilgrims were in stage 2 and not fully in stage 1 is that they were not generally being put to death. They did, however, experience extreme unwelcomeness in England. They were faced with heavy fines, incarceration, harassment, no freedom of press or speech, and ultimately were forced into hiding. Other like-minded Separatists, were, in fact, executed. The Pilgrims also saw a rapid decline down the "Spectrum of Welcome," as they moved from being tolerated and marginalized to demeaned, excluded, and closer towards and openly hostile environment.

Spectrum of Welcome: Pilgrims in the Netherlands Prior to Embarking on the Mayflower

1. Openly Hostile Environment	**2. Excluded**	**3. Demeaned**

4. Marginalized (not welcome)	**5. Allowed if conformed or assimilated** ←	**6. Differences Tolerated**

7. Differences Included	**8. Welcome**	**9. Celebrated**

When the Pilgrims fled England for the Netherlands, they encountered assimilation problems. While they were able to worship freely, they soon found that they were losing their English identity to the Dutch. It became clear that they would survive, but only if they were completely assimilated with the Dutch culture. English authorities also began to pressure authorities in the Netherlands to extradite their leaders, such as William Brewster, back to England to be prosecuted. The Dutch authorities began to cede to English rule and came looking for the Separatist leaders, which is why the chart is trending downwards towards stage 4: Marginalized.

Spectrum of Welcome: Pokanoket Wampanoag View of Pilgrims upon Initial Landing

1. Openly Hostile Environment	2. Excluded	3. Demeaned

4. Marginalized (not welcome)	5. Allowed if conformed or assimilated	6. Differences Tolerated

7. Differences Included	8. Welcome	9. Celebrated

The Pilgrim's initial landing at Cape Cod alarmed the native Pokanoket Wampanoag, which triggered an exchange of arrows and bullets. (No injuries or casualties resulted from this one incident.) After this encounter, the Pilgrims and Pokanoket Wampanoag had no contact for several months, but soon both groups would move to the opposite end of the "Spectrum of Welcome."

Spectrum of Welcome: Pokanoket Wampanoag View of Pilgrims after One Year

1. Openly Hostile Environment	2. Excluded	3. Demeaned

4. Marginalized (not welcome)	5. Allowed if conformed or assimilated	6. Differences Tolerated →

7. Differences Included →	8. Welcome →	9. Celebrated

Spectrum of Welcome: Pilgrim View of Pokanoket Wampanoag after One Year

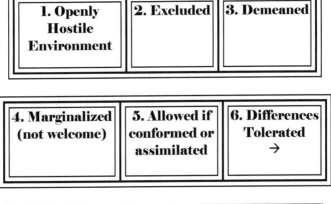

The relationship between the Pokanoket Wampanoag and the Pilgrims is a beautiful illustration of two completely different groups not only co-existing, but seeing to the survival and protection of the other group. The Pokanoket Wampanoag quickly went from simply tolerating their new neighbors to including them by teaching the Pilgrims how to properly hunt, fish, and grow crops. This led to a shared welcoming environment between the two groups. After a plentiful harvest, the Pilgrims and Pokanoket Wampanoag reached the pinnacle of the "Spectrum of Welcome" by *celebrating* with one another in unison in the most welcoming environment.

Spectrum of Welcome: Christians in America at its Founding

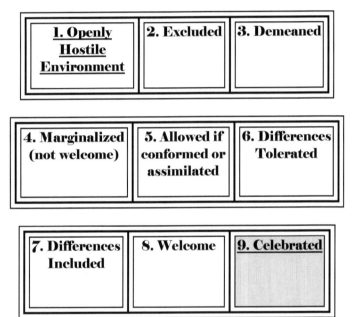

1. Openly Hostile Environment	**2. Excluded**	**3. Demeaned**

4. Marginalized (not welcome)	**5. Allowed if conformed or assimilated**	**6. Differences Tolerated**

7. Differences Included	**8. Welcome**	**9. Celebrated**

Christianity had more than just a welcome home in America at its birth as a nation: it served as the cornerstone for the underlying principles, values, doctrines, and morals that would eventually help propel America to become the leading world power. The Founding Fathers knew and understood freedom of religion as the most important freedom, and therefore Christianity was more than just welcomed, it was celebrated.

Spectrum of Welcome: Christians in America in 1950

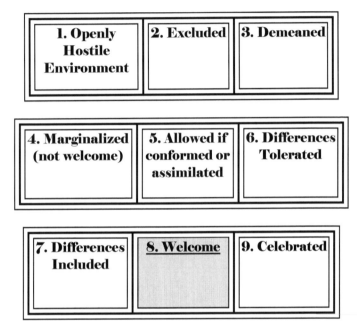

1. Openly Hostile Environment	2. Excluded	3. Demeaned
4. Marginalized (not welcome)	5. Allowed if conformed or assimilated	6. Differences Tolerated
7. Differences Included	8. Welcome	9. Celebrated

Christians in America had little to worry about in 1950 in the area of religion. The two-parent, husband and wife family unit was strong, religious freedom was still alive and well, America was booming, and Christianity was welcome.

Spectrum of Welcome: Christians in America in 2008

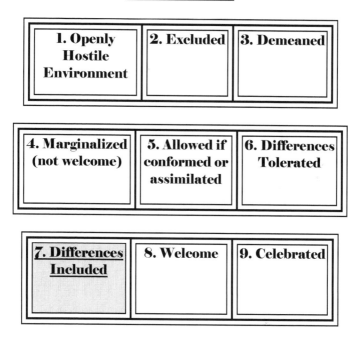

1. Openly Hostile Environment	2. Excluded	3. Demeaned

4. Marginalized (not welcome)	5. Allowed if conformed or assimilated	6. Differences Tolerated

7. Differences Included	8. Welcome	9. Celebrated

By 2008, Christians in America were not living in the same environment they once knew. Religious liberty did not appear to be in the dire condition it is today, but it was clear that being a Christian was becoming less welcomed.

Spectrum of Welcome: Christians in America in 2012

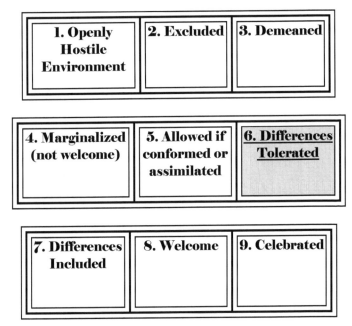

1. Openly Hostile Environment	2. Excluded	3. Demeaned

4. Marginalized (not welcome)	5. Allowed if conformed or assimilated	6. Differences Tolerated

7. Differences Included	8. Welcome	9. Celebrated

The attitude in America seemed to shift to: "If you're a Christian, Ok, but keep it to yourself." There appeared to be a growing resentment towards Christianity and any reference to God in the public square. The culture in America increasingly wanted little to do with Christianity or outspoken Christians, and attacks on religious liberty were underway.

Spectrum of Welcome: Christians in America Today

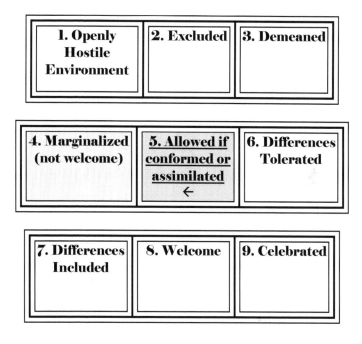

1. Openly Hostile Environment	2. Excluded	3. Demeaned

4. Marginalized (not welcome)	5. Allowed if conformed or assimilated ←	6. Differences Tolerated

7. Differences Included	8. Welcome	9. Celebrated

Believing in the Bible and living out the Christian faith in accordance with God's word in one's everyday life is no longer acceptable by society's standards. Christians can't believe in traditional marriage without being called bigots and hatemongers, abstinence is laughed at, truth is whatever people want it to be, and somehow, the belief that all life is precious and worth saving has to be defended. The government continues to encroach on religious freedom, as evidenced by the mounting number of cases listed in the previous chapter, and Christian business owners are being forced to choose between their faith and life's work.

Christians in America are finding themselves on increasingly marginalized ground. The only way Christians can be socially and culturally acceptable, and acceptable to the government, is if they conform to what the rest of the world says is fitting.

Spectrum of Welcome: Christians in America in 2020?

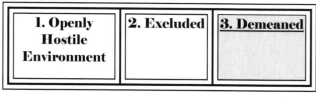

1. Openly Hostile Environment	2. Excluded	3. Demeaned

4. Marginalized (not welcome) ←	5. Allowed if conformed or assimilated	6. Differences Tolerated

7. Differences Included	8. Welcome	9. Celebrated

What will the state of Christianity in America be in 2020, the 400th anniversary of the sailing of the *Mayflower* to the New World? We know that religious liberty and the Christian faith are being attacked as it becomes increasingly marginalized. If things continue this way, and the wrong person is sitting in the office of the President of the United States, Christians in America will continue to watch their faith be trampled on and their religious freedoms crushed.

The Pilgrims experienced a tumble down the "Spectrum of Welcome" similar to what Christians are starting to go through in America today.

Simply put, Christians in America are no longer being welcomed.

CHAPTER FIVE

Marriage Equality has nothing to do with Marriage Equality

"I believe that marriage is the union between a man and a woman. Now, for me as a Christian . . . as a Christian, it is also a sacred union. God's in the mix." ~Barack Obama, speaking to Rick Warren's Saddleback Church in 2008[74]

The two-parent family unit is the basis for society–and it is broken. Many people hear this phrase, "the family is the basis for society," and brush it off as merely a cliché, but this phrase isn't a cliché, it's profound. We know that children need parents; they need one mom and one dad.[75]

The family unit was the most important structure to the Pilgrims in founding Plymouth Colony, just as it was to the Founding Fathers and just as it has been throughout not only American history, but world history, until today. As the basis of society, the family unit should be and needs to be supported, but instead it is being undermined in more ways than one.

Unquestionably, the issue of homosexuality, marriage equality, and the legalization of gay marriage in the United States has put the church at odds with the government and jeopardized religious freedom. When the United States Supreme Court imposed its will on the nation and officially redefined marriage, they were not creating marriage equality, because the right for homosexuals to marry isn't really about homosexuals being able to marry.

That's right, the push for marriage equality has *almost nothing to do with actual marriage equality*. Few people understand what is really going on. How is it that the issue of gay marriage and marriage equality went from a bipartisan non-issue to the forefront of almost every political and societal debate and discussion in the matter of only a year? It is now to the point where if one even so much as supports traditional marriage, they are considered a bigot who hates gay people. The degree to which the gay marriage agenda has progressed in such a short span of time at the expense of religious liberty is truly astonishing. If it seems as if it is being shoved down our throats, it's because it is.

Liberal progressives running the mainstream media and in top government positions don't really care about gays being able to get married. They want to silence the Christians who oppose them. The issue with legalizing gay marriage and so-called marriage equality is about more than just undermining the traditional family structure and God's intent for marriage; Christian schools, groups, organizations, non-profits, and even churches and ministers who try to proclaim the gospel and do not fully support the legalization of gay marriage will lose tax-exempt status, accreditation, necessary credentials, and face harassment from the government, all because they do not support gay marriage. Once this happens, these schools and organizations will start closing their doors and lose all ability to do good works, service, and proclaim the gospel.

The United States Department of Education sets the standards and guidelines that decide how schools and universities receive accreditation. With gay marriage now "a fundamental right," Christian schools and universities that do not embrace gay marriage are now in grave danger of losing accreditation and tax-exempt status. Private education is already costly. How many people do you think will continue to pay the price for private Christian education when the school is not accredited and prices rise dramatically to account for the loss of tax-exempt status? Homeschools could easily suffer the same fate. This means Christian education may cease to operate. What happens next? Churches, too, will become a target, losing tax exempt status as pastors are fined and jailed for committing offenses against the state.

Gay marriage as the law of the land could eventually mean that any pastor who refuses to marry a same-sex couple is breaking the law, and is therefore susceptible to fines and jail time. The intent is for Christianity to lose its voice and influence in America. Any organization, be it church, school, or non-profit, that does not support same-sex marriage or the edicts flowing from this new constitutional right can now be treated the same as an organization that engages in racism, all because they are in opposition to the United States government and hold to the belief that marriage was created by God with the intent that it is to remain between one man and one woman.

Christians cannot stop homosexuals from being homosexual against their will, nor should they, as that is every individual's personal business alone. The government cannot force a homosexual to attend or participate in a religious ceremony that teaches homosexuality is a sin. So why is it, then, that the government has decided they can force a privately owned business to participate in a homosexual marriage ceremony? The answer is that mandating recognition of gay marriage is not just about achieving marriage equality. The courts are now defining what faith should look like, how it should be practiced, and what Americans can believe in, subsequently pitting the church, Christian schools, universities, organizations, and conservative Christians against the government.

*****

The Pilgrims did not encounter this specific issue of having their government pressure them to accept gay marriage, but they did experience issues revolving around private property and a government that wanted to dictate their beliefs and practices. The homosexual and marriage equality activists' argument comes down to a central point that says they have a right to other individual's labor and property all because they have certain sexual rights that trump religious freedom. You will bake the cake, you will take the photographs, you will provide the flowers, and you will conduct the ceremony, etc., they say, because they have certain sexual rights. If you don't comply, you will be fined thousands upon thousands of dollars, face potential jail time, and possibly even lose your business. What kind of backwards ideology is this? This isn't necessarily even a religious freedom issue, but simply a freedom issue.

Christian bakers, florists, photographers and pastors are American citizens, and no one has a right to their private property or labor–certainly not because of their sexual orientation. Under no circumstances should the government force anyone to participate in a religious ceremony (or what may be viewed as a sacrilegious mockery of one) if they do not want to.

The theology of the husband-wife union and of marriage is not some inconsequential concept in Christianity. It is, in fact, a central tenant. The Church is the symbolic bride of Christ, and forcing Christians to participate in homosexual ceremonies is a desecration of their faith. This point may have been lost on Justice Anthony Kennedy, but certainly not on the Christian community.

Yes, marriage is about love, but it is also about a social structure which creates stability for children.

The United States government didn't invent marriage, period. Marriage is God's deal–He designed it. Marriage has been one man and one woman from the beginning. It is not a creature of the government; it is a covenant before God, and the government does not have the right to change that.[76] The United States government originally got in the business of marriage to establish protection for women and children.[77] How far we have strayed from that model.

We have lost what it means to be married, and this is not just a Christian issue, but a societal issue–and it is not just because of homosexuality and gay activists, but because of no-fault divorce and the separation of marriage and sex.[78] No-fault divorce has led to a dramatic increase in divorce rates as well as a plunge in marriage rates across the country. Ronald Reagan, who signed the No-Fault Divorce legislation into law as governor of California, later identified it as a serious issue and a major mistake, saying it was "one of the worst mistakes I ever made in public office."[79]

During the sexual revolution of the 1960s and 1970s, sex was separated from marriage. This ultimately led to childbearing being separated from marriage, and now men and women are being made completely interchangeable in marriage. These ideas are not just being accepted, but pushed and applauded as good and true in our society. This is harmful ideology because it is contrary to God's design and requires heavy propaganda and force to maintain. It is a dangerous and pagan ideology, which is why it is not an issue that Christians can just ignore or conform to.[80]

The redefinition of marriage as whatever anyone wants it to be will end up completely exchanging kinship with a combination of contracts and a welfare state, which will in time lead to abolishing marriage. This is no farce; "husband and wife," as well as "father and mother," are already being removed from government legal documents as the nation moves towards genderless parenting.[81] As previously mentioned, it has gotten to the point where in California you can longer be "husband and wife", just spouse 1 and spouse 2.[82]

It must be emphasized that lesbians and gays aren't targets or projects, they're our neighbors and our friends. We must not take a posture *against* them; we must take a posture *for human flourishing*. This means protecting and promoting marriage as it was designed and intended by God.[83] It's what the Pilgrims did, it's what the Founding Fathers did, and it's what we must do a better job of today.

The Pilgrims didn't conform to their corrupt national church and government, which wanted to tell them what they could and couldn't preach and believe, what was right and what was wrong, what was their private property and what no longer was. Instead, they chose to stand in the truth, as Christians in America must do once more today.

CHAPTER SIX

America: Land of the Free ... Abortion

"We hold these truths to be self-evident, that all men are created equal, that they are endowed by their Creator with certain unalienable Rights, that among these are Life, Liberty and the pursuit of Happiness."
~United States of America Declaration of Independence

Here's a question that many people struggle to answer: Is abortion legal through all nine months of pregnancy in the United States? Some might say no, it can only be during the first trimester, only through second trimester, or it depends on the state. The correct answer? Yes, legally, a mother may have her baby aborted at any time during her pregnancy, even up to nine months, because of the health exception in *Doe v. Bolton* (which accompanied *Roe v. Wade*), establishing that an abortion is legal at any point up to the actual birth of the baby as long as any one physician who is willing to perform the abortion says it is necessary for "the preservation of the ... health of the mother."[84]

Protecting the life of the mother certainly appears to be a worthy cause. However, here is what "health" constitutes according to the ruling in *Doe v. Bolton*: the "stigma of unwed motherhood, the work of 'child care,' and the distress, for all concerned, associated with the unwanted child."[85]

Those who find themselves on the pro-life side of the abortion debate are often labeled as extremists, but really, with abortion being legal through all nine months of pregnancy in America, for as simple of a reason as "distress," and the fact it can be funded by tax dollars, America has as radical and extreme of an abortion law as anywhere in the world.[86]

The legality of something doesn't change what it is, and it doesn't change its moral or ethical component. Cultures can promote life or cultures can promote death, they can enable human flourishing or they can suppress it.[87] The culture in America isn't promoting life and enabling human flourishing, it is destroying it.

Abortion is a sensitive issue, but refusing to accept the idea that the right of a mother to kill her child is greater than the right for the child to live, or refusing to believe that it is empowering for a woman to have the ability to end the life of her unborn child–a child with its own DNA and heartbeat, does not constitute a "war on women." When abortion became legal in the United States in 1973, it was done under the guise that it would be "safe and rare." Safe and rare? Abortion is a violent procedure that ends the life of the unborn child, and has now taken place more than 55 million times.[88] Not exactly a safe or rare procedure.

No one should be saying that abortion is just a women's issue, as abortion affects our entire society. Roughly 1/6th of a generation in America is missing–they have been destroyed and wiped away. If anyone still wants to cling to the argument that abortion is solely a women's issue, then perhaps they should remember the more than 25 million baby boys who were never given a chance to live and had their right to life denied, or the fathers who wanted to keep their baby, but whose voices were ignored. Roughly half of our population isn't female, but one shouldn't have to be a woman to voice their opinion on the atrocity that is legalized abortion. Reasonable people with a heart, a brain, and half a conscience can see that taking the life of an unborn baby is immoral, evil, and nothing but a giant lie masked by the abortion industry under the false narrative that abortion is "empowering."

What has been the result of the "empowerment of women" by abortion? 200+ million women are missing across the world.[89] How about that for empowerment? America must value human life, not destroy it. Abortion hasn't empowered women, it has failed them.

No one should ever have to apologize for standing up for life. Civil society should not allow the intentional killing of an unborn child simply because it is an inconvenience.[90] What if we had a culture and society that supported life, not undermined it? We need a culture that wraps its arms around a woman facing a crisis pregnancy and that encourages them to choose life. We need a government that says, instead of paying for you to have an abortion and end the life of your child, we will pay for you to birth the child and find a family to place it with that will love your child. Would that be such a bad thing–to have a government and culture that fosters life, not death?

Science is continuing to show us that an unborn child inside the womb is not a blob of cells or a potential life, but a distinct human being, separate from its parents with its own DNA and heartbeat. From the earliest stages of development, you were a distinct, living, whole human being. Each of us has the same human DNA that we have had since we were an embryo.[91] Our laws should reflect scientific reality; we must start recognizing that unborn life is not just potential life, rather that it IS life *with* potential.[92]

The left needs to start answering the question of when life begins. Instead of posing all sorts of hypothetical questions to pro-life people, what if pro-choice activists actually had to answer specific questions, such as when does life begin, if not at conception?

If it's when the baby is born, what is different about the development of the baby in the moments after it is born compared to moments before it is born, when it is still susceptible to abortion? Nothing- the only thing that changed is the baby's location.

Those who won't accept the fact that an unborn child is exactly that– a child–and say, "we don't know when life begins," or "we don't know that the unborn are human," need to be asked, "if we don't know, should we really be killing them?" If you're driving down a street at night and you see a baby stroller in the middle of the road, do you steamroll it and hope there's no baby inside, or do you take every precaution to avoid bringing any possible harm?

One need not even start the moral argument over abortion concerning God. The key question is simple: What is the status of the "unborn creature" in the womb? This is not a theological question. Is it a human being or isn't it? If so, doesn't it deserve to have the same right to life as the doctors in the room?[93] Again, the science is clear: from the earliest stages of development, the unborn are a distinct, living, whole human being.

Everyone alive today and everyone who has ever lived in the history of the world was at some point at the same stage of development as when the unborn are being aborted. What if you had been aborted when you were still in the womb? You wouldn't be here to argue about abortion. Abortion stops a beating heart and brings death, not empowerment.

*****

America is not at its best when we are killing our weakest and most vulnerable citizens.[94] What does it say about our nation when our elected officials can't come to terms with the idea that we should support a culture of life, not death, and can't even agree to stop sending tax payer dollars to an organization (Planned Parenthood) that is dismembering the unborn and harvesting their organs to sell for profit?

Don't hold your breath for the liberal media and liberal politicians to finally come to grips with what abortion really is, and what it is doing to our nation. They would have us believe abortion is a wonderful thing that should be readily available to all woman at any point in their pregnancy, for any reason. And if you oppose that point of view you are an out-of-touch extremist who hates women. Why does being pro-life mean one hates women? Because they don't want millions of little girl's lives' to be terminated?

Take a look at what some of the most influential women in history have said about abortion:

❖ "It will burden her conscience in life, it will burden her soul in death; but oh, thrice guilty is he who…drove her to the desperation which impelled her to the crime."
~Susan B. Anthony[95]

❖ "When we consider that women are treated as property, it is degrading to women that we should treat our children as property to be disposed of as we wish."
~Elizabeth Cady Stanton[96]

❖ "America needs no words from me to see how your decision in *Roe v. Wade* has deformed a great nation. The so-called right to abortion has pitted mothers against their children and women against men."
~Mother Teresa[97]

❖ "Abortion kills twice. It kills the body of the baby and it kills the

conscience of the mother. Abortion is profoundly anti-women. Three quarters of its victims are women: Half the babies and all the mothers."
~Mother Teresa[98]

❖ "Abortion is the ultimate exploitation of women."
~Alice Paul[99]

Compare these quotes with those of Margaret Sanger, founder of Planned Parenthood, the largest abortion provider in America:

❖ "The most merciful thing that the large family does to one of its infant members is to kill it."[100]

❖ "[We should] apply a stern and rigid policy of sterilization and segregation to that grade of population whose progeny is tainted, or whose inheritance is such that objectionable traits may be transmitted to offspring."[101]

❖ "Give dysgenic groups [people with "bad genes"] in our population their choice of segregation or [compulsory] sterilization."[102]

Today, there are more people working full time to kill babies than there are working to save them. For all of the reasons discussed above, this is a serious problem.[103] Outside of sharing the gospel, abortion is the most important issue of our time, and we know far too much to continue to sit idly by.

Once again, it is time for America to face itself in the mirror, and perhaps look closer at the story of the Pilgrims and their voyage to the New World. America needs a culture of life and a government that supports that culture. This is what the Pilgrims established for their colony, both in the New World and on the *Mayflower*.

During the Pilgrim's journey on the *Mayflower*, one child was born during the voyage across the Atlantic Ocean. If you want to talk about the health of the mother being jeopardized, distressful circumstances, and a crisis pregnancy, look no further. On a dirty, cramped, crowded, and moving ship, full of sick and hungry people, Elizabeth Hopkins gave birth to her first son while at sea and named him Oceanus.[104] After the

Mayflower arrived in New England, a second baby boy, Peregrine White, was born to Susanna White.[105]

Far from ideal circumstances to bear a child, even in those times, the Pilgrims welcomed, supported, and celebrated this new life. Why is this important? Because at the time of these two births, the babies were nothing but an extreme inconvenience and hindrance to the Pilgrims. It meant two more mouths to feed, two more bodies to clothe and shelter, and two more lives to care for everyday, which could not provide any benefit to the rest of the colony for years. The birth of these babies placed a heavier burden on the already tired and weary Pilgrims. If the mothers of these babies were in modern day America, would they be told to do themselves and everyone else a favor and terminate the pregnancy? Or would the new life be welcomed and celebrated as a joyous occasion, like the Pilgrims did at the actual births?

The Pilgrims did what many today refuse to do, and that is to see the unborn for what they really are: a new life that should be welcomed and supported. If the Pilgrims knew this in the 1620s, with no modern scientific evidence or technology, shouldn't America today do the same?

CHAPTER SEVEN

Religious Liberty or Ambiguous Bigotry?

"It cannot be emphasized too strongly or too often that this great nation was founded, not by religionists, but by Christians; not on religions, but on the gospel of Jesus Christ. For this very reason peoples of other faiths have been afforded asylum, prosperity, and freedom of worship here."
~ Patrick Henry[106]

In the ongoing debate surrounding religious liberty, people on both sides of the argument of all beliefs, faiths, and backgrounds should be asking the same question: Does the censorship of religion promote the abundant life, or weaken it?

The answer is simple, the censorship of religion undermines citizens' most important beliefs and jeopardizes a spectrum of freedoms for all. This same question was placed in front of the Pilgrims, who ultimately reached this same conclusion that many are missing today: that religious freedom is the most important and essential freedom for living the abundant life. The Pilgrims went to great lengths and overcame grave circumstances in pursuit of religious freedom–an important example that needs to be remembered today.

Keep in mind, people who believe in same-sex marriage should absolutely have the right to believe that. Equivalently, no one has a right to dictate anyone else's religious beliefs. No one in the LGBT community can be forced into participating in a religious ceremony, and no Muslim can be forced to adhere to Jewish ceremonial law, or vice versa.

Traditional marriage, the lifelong union of one man and one woman, guarantees that more children will be raised in a loving, stable home by both a mother and a father. Having a mom and a dad is a distinctive need that every child has, and this need deserves to be fulfilled. Today, however, if you believe this–the same thing that has been almost universally taught since the dawn of man, or that intentionally designing fatherless or motherless homes is bad public policy, you are labeled a bigot and intolerant.

Conservatives and Christians must start appealing to shared values: freedom of expression, diversity, and tolerance as a two-way street. The American Christian has rights, the American atheist has rights, the Christian baker has rights, and the gay florist has rights. This idea of tolerance being a two way street has been turned in to a one-way road for trampling religious freedom.

For instance, a "GoFundMe" page was created for the "Sweet Cakes by Melissa" bakery, after the owners of the bakery were struck with a $135,000 fine for refusing to bake a wedding cake for a lesbian couple. GoFundMe had the page for the bakery taken down and said they weren't going to allow the bakery to raise money through their site.[107] Based on their moral values and beliefs, they made a decision to not provide their services or allow Sweet Cakes to raise money through their business, just like the Sweet Cakes bakery made a faith-based decision. However, only one group was fined $135,000.

*****

Consider the following quote from radio host, author, and political commentator Tammy Bruce, who identifies as lesbian:

> My friendships and relationships in the conservative world are not predicated on political correctness and enforced conformity of thought. They are based, instead, on mutual respect, honesty and understanding–concepts many modern liberals should consider revisiting.

This illustrates an important point and demonstrates why, when religious freedom starts being compromised, it is dangerous for all. What happens when you diminish religious liberty and drive out Christianity and the idea that civil liberties and freedoms come from God, not man? The state becomes the source of all rights.[108]

If the current trends and government actions that undermine Christianity continue to progress, the United States government itself will become the great source of all rights. This is why the censorship of religion undermines citizens' most important beliefs and jeopardizes a spectrum of freedoms not just for Christians, but for all.

The Pilgrims took a stand for religious freedom that we must mirror again today. Everyone, particularly leaders in our churches, communities, and government, need to remember the likes of Pilgrim Elder William Brewster, who at a time when men's life spans were far shorter than today, left Europe to face the terrible hardships of starting a new colony at the age of 53–all in order to seek out religious freedom in America. It is time, again, to seek out religious freedom in America.

CHAPTER EIGHT

Choosing the *Right* Rock

"He who wants to win the world for Christ must have the courage to come in conflict with it."
~ Titus Brandsma[109]

We are losing something. Our society is moving from Western Christendom to something else. Up until around the 1960s, one could say America was a Christian nation.[110] People can't say that anymore. So what is our calling in these challenging times, when our nation moves from welcoming Christians to open hostility towards Christians? It is to be an image of God.

The things which God loves, we should love also. We must not be fearful, and we cannot give in to fear, or we will sound hateful to the world.[111] America is entering into a phase that will require many to be faced with the choice between their Christian faith and their job. For those who are serious about their Christian faith, it is a great opportunity to change the small things.[112]

America needs Christianity. Christians and conservatives must do a better job of engaging with our culture. Read, study, and equip yourself to engage in the battles that lie ahead. Much of this needs to occur in–and then flow out from–the church. Pastors must start waking up their congregations to take action outside of just their church walls. Political and cultural battles are intertwined with religion, whether one desires it or not, and Christians must be involved.

For instance, how many Christians do you think voted in the 2012 election cycle? What if I told you it was less than half? In the aftermath of the 2012 election, according to *The Blaze*,

> The U.S. Census says there are more than 311 million people in the United States. If evangelical adults are 26

percent of them, then there would be 80 million potential voters.

So far, 123 million votes have been counted in this election–and that number will get higher by the millions as votes continue to be counted like in 2008. Evangelicals made up 26 percent of them, therefore, about 32 million evangelicals voted–less than half of their population.[113]

Rev. Franklin Graham has taken note of this, stating:

We know that from of the statistics that I've heard that the majority of Christians in this country just did not vote for whatever reason, the vast majority of evangelicals did not go to the polls. God is in control, and if Christians are upset, they need to be upset at themselves. We need to do a better job of getting our people- the church to vote. Now, I'm not trying to tell you how to vote, you can vote, but vote, my goodness, and vote for candidates that stand for Biblical values.[114]

Churches cannot and should not explicitly tell people how to vote, but that doesn't mean they are incapable of pointing people in the right direction to find the necessary resources with the information people need to make an informed vote that reflects their values. This needs to happen not just for the Presidential election, but at state, city, county, and school board levels.

The star of the film *God's Not Dead*, Kevin Sorbo, sums it up well:

> Seventy-five percent of Christians… didn't even vote in the last two elections. Well, you know what? You get the government you deserve. You've got to get out there. Pastors have got to wake their congregations up. You can't sit there and say that religion and politics shouldn't be mixed—of course they're mixed. This country was founded on Christianity, for crying out loud.[115]

The Pilgrims landed at Plymouth Rock, but more importantly, they built on Christ the Rock. What will Christians in America today choose for their rock? Republicans? Democrats? The Bible tells us that "The heart of the wise inclines to the right, but the heart of the fool to the left."[116] Pun intended. However, ultimately Christians in America must look to God, not just politicians.

Christians must act out of love, but they still have the right to stand up for themselves, their values, and for the betterment of society. Too many people have sacrificed too much for religious freedom to let it go by the wayside in America. When the mayor of Houston, Annise Parker, attempted to subpoena five pastors, the far-reaching backlash she received from across the county forced her to retract the subpoenas and keep the government's hands off of the pulpit.

The original significance of separation of Church and State was not to prevent Christians from expressing their faith in public, but to keep the government from hindering the free exercise of religion and imposing state religion like the one the Pilgrims fled. The Pilgrims recognized this long before it was written in U.S. law, and it must be recognized again today.

2020 will mark the 400th anniversary of the Pilgrims' arrival in America. It is time for Christians, and people of all faiths, to join in the fight to preserve the religious freedom that Pilgrims came to find on American soil, so that once again our nation will be one that promotes and establishes religious freedom as the key that holds together all freedoms for all people.

Bibliography

Introduction

----

[1] Plimoth Plantation. *Smithsonian Institute Affiliations Program*. "Who Were the Pilgrims?" (http://www.plimoth.org/learn). Retrieved 12 June 2015.

[2] Atkins, Scott. *University of Virginia*, A work completed for the "Capitol Project," from the *American Studies* group. "Salem Witchcraft." (http://xroads.virginia.edu/~CAP/puritan/purhist.html). Retrieved 12 June 2015.

[3] Van Der Woude, Joanne. "Plymouth Colony." *Britain and The Americas: Culture, Politics, and History*. Santa Barbara: ABC-CLIO, 2005. (http://search.credoreference.com/content/topic/plymouth_colony). Retrieved 16 June 2015.

Chapter One

[4] Inspirational Quotes. 2015.
(http://www.inspirationallquotes.com/robert-agostinelli-quotes-about-life-good-political-2/).

[5] Plimoth Plantation. *Smithsonian Institute Affiliations Program*. "Who Were the Pilgrims?" (http://www.plimoth.org/learn). Retrieved 12 June 2015.

[6] Atkins, Scott. *University of Virginia*, A work completed for the "Capitol Project," from the *American Studies* group. "The Puritans." (http://xroads.virginia.edu/~CAP/puritan/purhist.html). Retrieved 12 June 2015.

[7] Plimoth Plantation. *Smithsonian Institute Affiliations Program.*

[8] The Elizabeth Files. "Act of Uniformity 1559." (http://www.elizabethfiles.com/act-of-uniformity-1559/3833/). Accessed 16 June 2015.

[9] Plimoth Plantation. *Smithsonian Institute Affiliations Program.*

[10] "Brewster, William". *Encyclopædia Britannica* (11 Ed.). Cambridge University Press. 1911.

[11] Plimoth Plantation. *Smithsonian Institute Affiliations Program.*

[12] Griffis, William. P. 575. "The Pilgrim Press in Leyden." *New England Magazine* (Boston: Warren F. Kellogg). 19/25 (January 1899): 559-575. (http://ebooks.library.cornell.edu/cgi/t/text/pageviewer-idx?c=newe;cc=newe;rgn=full%20text;idno=newe0025-5;didno=newe0025-5;view=image;seq=00567;node=newe0025-5%3A1). Accessed 12 June 2015.

[13] Atkins, Scott. "The Pilgrims." (http://xroads.virginia.edu/~CAP/puritan/purhist.html).

[14] Ibid.

[15] Plimoth Plantation. *Smithsonian Institute Affiliations Program.*

[16] Ames, Azel. *The Mayflower and her Log.* New York: Houghton, Miflin (1907). (http://www.gutenberg.org/files/4107/4107-h/4107-h.htm). Accessed 12 June 2015.

[17] Plimoth Plantation. *Smithsonian Institute Affiliations Program.*

[18] Atkins, Scott. "Thanksgiving and the Indians." (http://xroads.virginia.edu/~CAP/puritan/purhist.html).

[19] Ibid.

[20] Ibid.

[21] Ibid.

[22] Plimoth Plantation. *Smithsonian Institute Affiliations Program.*

[23] Atkins, Scott. "The Mayflower Compact." (http://xroads.virginia.edu/~CAP/puritan/purhist.htm)

[24] George Ernest Bowman. "The Mayflower Compact and its Signers. Boston: Massachusetts Society of Mayflower Descendants, 1920. (http://ia802306.us.archive.org/0/items/mayflowercompact00bow/mayflowercompact00bow.pdf).

[25] RLROUSE Directory & Informational Resources. "The Mayflower Compact." (This interpretation of The Mayflower Compact is courtesy of Dep. Alfa-Informatica University of Groningen, 2014.) (http://www.rlrouse.com/mayflower-compact.html).

[26] Atkins, Scott. "The Mayflower Compact." (http://xroads.virginia.edu/~CAP/puritan/purhist.htm)

[27] Plimoth Plantation. *Smithsonian Institute Affiliations Program.*

[28] Ibid.

[29] Atkins, Scott. "Excursus: Henry Cabot Lodge and the Plymouth Tercentenary." (http://xroads.virginia.edu/~CAP/puritan/purtrad.html#lodge).

[30] Ibid.

[31] Lodge, Henry Cabot. "The Pilgrims of Plymouth." The Senate of the United States, and Other Essays and Addresses Historical and Literary. New York: Charles Scribner's Sons, 1921.

[32] Atkins, Scott. "Excursus: Henry Cabot Lodge and the Plymouth Tercentenary." (http://xroads.virginia.edu/~CAP/puritan/purtrad.html#lodge).

[33] Starnes, Todd. "City of Houston demands pastors turn over sermons." Fox News. 14 Oct. 2014. (http://www.foxnews.com/opinion/2014/10/14/city-houston-demands-pastors-turn-over-sermons.html).

Chapter Two

[34] "Pilgrim." Dictionary.com. (http://dictionary.reference.com/browse/pilgrim). Retrieved 10 July, 2015.

[35] Star, Penny. "Pastor: 'I Never Thought' My Nation Would Persecute 'Bible-Believing' Christians." CNS News. (http://cnsnews.com/news/article/penny-starr/pastor-i-never-thought-my-nation-would-persecute-bible-believing-christians). Retrieved 10 July 2015.

[36] Ibid.

[37] Becker, Kyle. "RGIII Enters NFL Event with a 'Know Jesus' T-Shirt on the Right Way, Leaves with It Inside-Out." IJR Review. (http://www.ijreview.com/2014/09/178340-rgiii-wears-t-shirt-inappropriate-nfl-choice-make-flip-inside/). Retrieved 16 July 2015.

[38] Spiering, Charlie. "OBAMA AT NATIONAL PRAYER BREAKFAST: 'PEOPLE COMMITTED TERRIBLE DEEDS IN THE NAME OF CHRIST." Breitbart. Feb. 5, 2015. (http://www.breitbart.com/big-government/2015/02/05/obama-at-national-prayer-breakfast-people-committed-terrible-deeds-in-the-name-of-christ/). Retrieved 16 July 2015.

[39] Boyer, Dave. "Obama criticizes 'less-than-loving' Christians." The Washington Times. April 7, 2015. (http://www.washingtontimes.com/news/2015/apr/7/obama-criticizes-less-than-loving-christians-at-ea/?page=all). Retrieved July 16 2015.

[40] Ibid.

[41] "California governor signs bill replacing words 'husband' and 'wife' in state law." Fox News. July, 7, 2014. (http://www.foxnews.com/politics/2014/07/07/calif

ornia-bill-replacing-words-husband-wife-in-marriage-law-signed-by-gov/). Retrieved 16 July 2015.

[42] McClam, Erin. "Religious Freedom Restoration Act: What You Need to Know." NBC News. Mar. 30, 2015. (http://www.nbcnews.com/news/us-news/indiana-religious-freedom-law-what-you-need-know-n332491). Retrieved July 16 2015.

[43] Darcy, Oliver. "You'll Likely Be Offended at Who Bill Maher Just Called a 'Psychotic Mass Murderer'." The Blaze. Mar. 15, 2014. (http://www.theblaze.com/stories/2014/03/15/bill-maher-has-a-strong-message-for-christians-who-worship-psychotic-mass-murderer-god/). Retrieved July 16 2015.

[44] McSwain, Steve. "Why Nobody Wants to Go to Church Anymore." Huffington Post. Nov. 14, 2013. (http://www.huffingtonpost.com/steve-mcswain/why-nobody-wants-to-go-to_b_4086016.html). Retrieved July 16 2015.

[45] Hicks, Josh. "Did Obama deny rights to infants who survive abortion?" The Washington Post. Sept. 10, 2012. (http://www.washingtonpost.com/blogs/fact-checker/post/did-obama-vote-to-deny-rights-to-infant-abortion-survivors/2012/09/07/9852895a-f87d-11e1-8398-0327ab83ab91_blog.html). Retrieved July 16 2015.

Chapter Three

[46] Sanburn, Josh. "Houston's Pastors Outraged After City Subpoenas Sermons Over Transgender Bill." Time. Oct. 17, 2014. (http://time.com/3514166/houston-pastors-sermons-subpoenaed/). Retrieved 18 July 2015.

[47] Chumley, Cheryl. "Idaho city's ordinance tells pastors to marry gays or go to jail." The Washington Times. Oct. 20, 2014. (http://www.washingtontimes.com/news/2014/oct/20/idaho-citys-ordinance-tells-pastors-to-marry-gays-/). Retrieved 18 July 2015.

[48] Starnes, Todd. "The Christian purge has begun: Chaplains banned from preaching that homosexuality is a sin." Fox News.com. Aug. 11, 2015. (http://www.foxnews.com/opinion/2015/08/11/chaplains-banned-from-preaching-that-homosexuality-is-sin.html?intcmp=hplnws). Retrieved 17 Aug. 2015.

[49] Grasz, Nate. "Would the Pilgrims want to come to America today?" Allen B. West.com. Nov. 27, 2014. (http://allenbwest.com/2014/11/pilgrims-want-come-america-today/). Retrieved 18 July 2015.

[50] Ibid.

[51] Ibid.

[52] "Denver court rules against Little Sisters of the Poor in contraception coverage case." Fox News. Jul. 15, 2015. (http://www.foxnews.com/politics/2015/07/15/denver-court-rules-against-little-sisters-poor-contraception-coverage-case/). Retrieved 18 July 2015.

[53] Starnes, Todd. "Christian bakers fined $135,000 for refusing to make wedding cake for lesbians." Fox News. Jul. 2, 2015. (http://www.foxnews.com/opinion/2015/07/02/christian-bakers-fined-135000-for-refusing-to-make-wedding-cake-for-lesbians.html). Retrieved 18 July 2015.

[54] Bigelow, William. "MISSOURI COMMISSION REMOVES DESERT STORM MEMORIAL WITH 'JESUS FISH'." Breitbart.com. Aug. 12, 2015. (http://www.breitbart.com/big-government/2015/08/12/missouri-commission-removes-desert-storm-memorial-with-jesus-fish/?utm_source=facebook&utm_medium=social). Retrieved 17 Aug. 2015.

[55] McConnell, Mitch. "The IRS scandal and Obama's culture of intimidation." The Washington Post. May 22, 2013. (http://www.washingtonpost.com/opinions/mitch-mcconnell-the-irs-scandal-and-obamas-culture-of-intimidation/2013/05/22/9c4b7de6-c2f8-11e2-914f-a7aba60512a7_story.html). Retrieved 18 July 2015.

[56] Blumer. Tom. "Not News: Obama Admin Admits Tax-Exempt Status of Churches at Stake in Supremes' Gay 'Marriage Case." April 30, 2015. Media Research Center. (http://newsbusters.org/blogs/tom-blumer/2015/04/30/not-news-obama-admin-admits-tax-exempt-status-non-complying-churches). Retrieved 18 July 2015.

[57] Grasz, Nate. "Would the Pilgrims want to come to America today?" Allen B. West.com. Nov. 27, 2014. (http://allenbwest.com/2014/11/pilgrims-want-come-america-today/). Retrieved 18 July 2015.

[58] "Undeniable: The Survey of Hostility to Religion in America." Liberty Institute. Plano, Texas: 2014.

(https://www.libertyinstitute.org/document.doc?id=22). Retrieved 18 July 2015.
[59] Carl, Michael. "PERSECUTION OF CHRISTIANS ON RISE – IN U.S." WND. Sep. 17, 2012. (http://www.wnd.com/2012/09/persecution-of-christians-on-rise-in-u-s/). Retrieved 18 July 2015.
[60] Ibid.
[61] Ibid.
[62] Ibid.
[63] Ibid.
[64] Ibid.
[65] Ibid.
[66] Ibid.
[67] Ibid.
[68] Ibid.
[69] Ibid.
[70] Grasz, Nate. "Would the Pilgrims want to come to America today?" Allen B. West.com. Nov. 27, 2014. (http://allenbwest.com/2014/11/pilgrims-want-come-america-today/). Retrieved 18 July 2015.
[71] Atkins, Scott. *University of Virginia*, A work completed for the "Capitol Project," from the *American Studies* group. "The Pilgrims in the Capitol." (http://xroads.virginia.edu/~CAP/puritan/purhist.html). Retrieved 20 July 2015.
[72] Ibid.

Chapter Four

[73] Edwards. Jeannie. "The Spectrum of Welcome." Lakewood, CO. 2015.

Chapter Five

[74] Miller, Zeke. "Axelrod: Obama Misled Nation When He Opposed Gay Marriage In 2008." Time.com. Feb. 10, 2015. (http://time.com/3702584/gay-marriage-axelrod-obama/). Retrieved 17 Aug. 2015.

[75] Morse, Jennifer. *Alliance Defending Freedom Collegiate Academy*. Aug. 13, 2015. Tucson, AZ.

[76] Ventrella, Jeffery. *Alliance Defending Freedom Collegiate Academy*. Aug. 13, 2015. Tucson, AZ.

[77] Morse, Jennifer. *Alliance Defending Freedom Collegiate Academy*. Aug. 13, 2015. Tucson, AZ.

[78] Ventrella, Jeffery. *Alliance Defending Freedom Collegiate Academy*. Aug. 13, 2015. Tucson, AZ.

[79] McManus, Michael. "Confronting the More Entrenched Foe: The Disaster of No-Fault Divorce and Its Legacy of Cohabitation." *The Family in America*. The Howard Center for Family, Religion, & Society, Rockford, Illinois, 2015.

[80] Morse, Jennifer. *Alliance Defending Freedom Collegiate Academy*. Aug. 13, 2015. Tucson, AZ.

[81] Ibid.

[82] Ventrella, Jeffery. *Alliance Defending Freedom Collegiate Academy*. Aug. 13, 2015. Tucson, AZ.

[83] Ibid.

Chapter Six

[84] Agresti, James. "Roe v. Wade allows abortions for all 9 months of pregnancy, not just the first 3." Just Facts Daily. Jan. 18, 2013. (http://www.justfactsdaily.com/roe-v-wade-allows-abortions-for-all-9-months-of-pregnancy-not-just-the-first-3/). Retrieved 18 Aug. 2015.

[85] Ibid.

[86] Nikas, Nikolas. *Alliance Defending Freedom Collegiate Academy*. Aug. 12, 2015. Tucson, AZ.

[87] Stonestreet, Josh. *Alliance Defending Freedom Collegiate Academy*. Aug. 10, 2015. Tucson, AZ.

[88] Ertelt, Steven. "55,772,015 Abortions in America Since Roe v. Wade in 1973." Life News.com. Jan. 18, 2013. (http://www.lifenews.com/2013/01/18/55772015-abortions-in-america-since-roe-vs-wade-in-1973/). Retrieved 18 Aug. 2015.

[89] Mattson, Brian. *Alliance Defending Freedom Collegiate Academy*. Aug. 11, 2015. Tucson, AZ.

[90] Klusendorf, Scott. *Alliance Defending Freedom Collegiate Academy*. Aug. 12. 2015. Tucson, AZ.

[91] Ibid.

[92] Nikas, Nikolas. *Alliance Defending Freedom Collegiate Academy*. Aug. 12, 2015. Tucson, AZ.

[93] Anderson, Ryan. *Alliance Defending Freedom Collegiate Academy*. Aug. 11, 2015. Tucson, AZ.

[94] West, Allen. *Western Conservative Summit 2014*. Denver, CO.

[95] Dannenfelser, Marjorie. "Early Suffragists." Susan B Anthony List. 2015. (http://www.sba-list.org/movement/notable-women/early-suffragists). Retrieved 18 Aug. 2015.

[96] Ibid.

[97] "Pro Life Quotations of Mother Teresa." Faithful Catholics. 2015. (https://sites.google.com/site/faithfulcatholics/Home/pro-life-quotations-of-mother-teresa). Retrieved 18 Aug. 2015.

[98] Ibid.

[99] Ibid.

[100] Enriquez, Lauren. "10-Eye-Opening Quotes From Planned Parenthood Founder Margaret Sanger." LifeNews.com. Mar. 11, 2013. (http://www.lifenews.com/2013/03/11/10-eye-opening-quotes-from-planned-parenthood-founder-margaret-sanger/). Retrieved 18 Aug. 2015.

[101] Ibid.

[102] Ibid.

[103] Klusendorf, Scott. *Alliance Defending Freedom Collegiate Academy*. Aug. 12. 2015. Tucson, AZ.

[104] "Mayflower and Mayflower Compact." Plimoth Planation. 2015. (http://www.plimoth.org/). Retrieved 18 Aug. 2015.

[105] Ibid.

Chapter Seven

[106] Fairchild, Marry. "Christian Quotes of the Founding Fathers." About.com. 2015. (http://christianity.about.com/od/independenceday/a/foundingfathers_3.htm). Retrieved 20 Aug. 2015.
[107] Sharp, Matt. *Alliance Defending Freedom Collegiate Academy*. Aug. 13, 2015. Tucson, AZ.
[108] Jeffrey, Ventrella. *Alliance Defending Freedom Collegiate Academy*. Aug. 12, 2015. Tucson, AZ.

Chapter Eight

[109] "Titus Brandsma." Society of Mt. Carmel. Carmelite Media. Darien, Illinois: 2015. (http://carmelnet.org/brandsma/). Retrieved 20 Aug. 2015.

[110] The inconsistency between Christianity and the treatment of racial minorities in America's past is not lost on the author. However, it was Christians like William Wilberforce and American abolitionists who worked to end slavery, and Christians like Reverend Dr. Martin Luther King Jr. who worked to end segregation and establish civil rights.

[111] Mattson, Brian. *Alliance Defending Freedom Collegiate Academy*. Aug. 11, 2015. Tucson, AZ.

[112] Baker, John. *Alliance Defending Freedom Collegiate Academy*. Aug. 11, 2015. Tucson, AZ.

[113] Hallowell, Billy. "Are Christians at Fault for Obama's Re-Election Win? Rev. Franklin Graham Says Yes." The Blaze. Nov. 19, 2012. (http://www.theblaze.com/stories/2012/11/19/are-christians-at-fault-for-obamas-re-election-win-rev-franklin-graham-says-yes/). Retrieved 22 Aug. 2015.

[114] Montanaro, Domenico. "No, it's not 'Christians'' fault Obama won." NBC News. Nov. 16, 2012. (http://firstread.nbcnews.com/_news/2012/11/16/15219396-no-its-not-christians-fault-obama-won?lite). Retrieved 22 August 2015.

[115] Hallowell, Billy. "Hollywood Actor: 'Pastors Have Got to Wake Their Congregations Up'." The Blaze. (http://www.theblaze.com/stories/2015/06/22/hollywood-actor-pastors-have-got-to-wake-their-congregations-up-if-they-want-to-fix-america/). Jun. 22, 2015. Retrieved 22 Aug, 2015.

[116] New International Version. Ecclesiastes 10:2.